HARCOURT SCHOOL PUBLISHERS

STORYtown

Balancing Act

D1360025

Brandon

Harcourt

SCHOOL PUBLISHERS

www.harcourtschool.com

ISBN 0-15-354536-4
ISBN 978-0-15-354536-8

12 13 14 15   1421   16 15 14 13 12 11
4500295199

CONTENTS

already

eight

police

prove

sign

Words to Know

Write the word that completes each sentence. The first one has been done for you.

1. "Look! A _____ **sign** _____ for hats!"

Pat went in to get a hat.

2. Pat sat with _____ cats.

3. "See my hat?" said Pat.

Pat _____ had his hat on.

4. Now Pat can't find his hat.

"The _____ can find it!"

Pat said.

5. Ann said she can find the hat.

She wants to _____

that she can.

Write the answers to these questions.
Use complete sentences.

6. What sign did Pat see?

_____

_____

7. What can Ann prove to Pat?

_____

_____

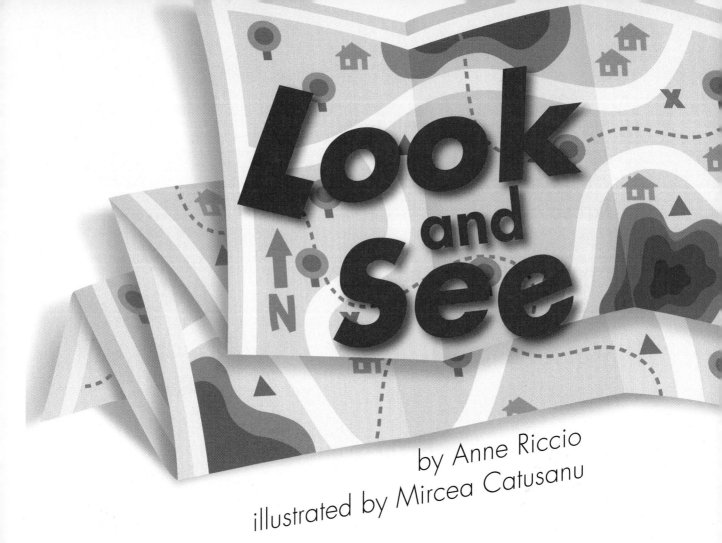

Look and See

by Anne Riccio

illustrated by Mircea Catusanu

Pat is sad.

"I can't find my hat," said Pat.

"I can find it," said Ann.

"Come on. We will look at a map.

Then we will find it."

Stop and Think

1 Why is Pat sad?

Pat is sad because ___He can't find___

___His hat.___

"Did you go in there?" asked Ann.

"I went to get my hat in there. Then I went in there," said Pat.

"I had my hat when I went in. I had it when I came out. We can go look. My hat is not there." **2**

Stop and Think

2 Where did Pat go after the hat store?

After the hat store, __back in the hat store.__

"Did you see Tad? Did you have it then?" asked Ann.

"No, I did not," said Pat. "But I saw Dan. I had my hat then." **3**

Stop and Think

3 Why is Ann asking Pat so many questions?

Ann is asking Pat many questions because _if she asks alot of questions that how the Hat._

"Were you in there?" Ann asked.

"I was," said Pat. "But I had my hat then. I had it when I sat with eight cats. I can prove it. We will look. You will see. It is not there." ④

Stop and Think

④ How will Pat prove that his hat is not in the library?

Pat will _look in the library._

"Can we go to the police now?"

"No," said Ann. "I said I can find it. I will find it." **5**

Stop and Think

5 What do Ann and Pat want to do now?

Ann wants to _find the hat by her self._

Pat wants to _go to the police._

"Did you go in there?" asked Ann.

"Yes. I had my hat then," said Pat.

"You came out. Did you have it then?"

"No," said Pat.

"Come on! We will go in. We will find
it," said Ann. **6**

Stop and Think

6 What do you think will happen next?

I think that ___they will find the hat.___

"Look! See that sign?"

"Yes," said Pat. "But I already went there. I did not find it."

"Look there!" said Ann. "Your hat is on the bag!" 7

Stop and Think

7 Do you think Ann is a good friend? Explain your answer.

I think Ann _is a good friend because she helped find pats hat._

Think Critically

1. What is the problem in the story? How is it solved? **PLOT**

The problem is that _____

_____

The problem is solved when _____

_____

2. How would you describe Pat? How would you describe Ann? Copy the chart and fill it in. **CHARACTERS**

Pat	Ann

3. What do you learn about friends from this story? **AUTHOR'S PURPOSE**

I learn that friends _____

_____

covered

everything

guess

through

woods

Write the word that completes each sentence. The first one has been done for you.

1. Pam and Stan run _____**through**_____ the woods.

2. Pam runs over _____ there.

3. Look! Stan is _____! What is all this on Stan?

4. Pam and Stan like to be in the _____.

5. Can you _____ what

they will find there?

Answer these questions. Use complete sentences.

6. Who runs through the woods?

_____

_____

7. What is Stan covered with?

_____

_____

8. What will they find in the woods?

_____

_____

GUESS WHAT WE HAVE

by Anne Riccio
illustrated by Barry Rockwell

"Look over there. We can go in there," says Pam. "Will Gram get mad? Will Gramps get mad?"

"No. We can be fast," says Stan.

Pam and Stan run in fast.

Stop and Think

1 What do you know about Stan and Pam so far?

Stan and Pam are ~~f~~ast runners.

HOME SWEET HOME

"Stan! Pam!" says Gram. "Come in.
Guess what we have!"
No Stan. No Pam.
Gramps runs into the woods. **2**

Stop and Think

2 What do you think Gramps will do?

I think he will _____

_____

"Look!" says Stan.

"Grab some!" says Pam. "Get some
for Gram. Get some for Gramps." **3**

Stop and Think

3 Why are they excited to find acorns?

They are excited to find acorns because _____

_____

They run fast through the woods.
Splat! Pam lands flat.

Stan goes to get Pam. But he cannot
stand up. Splat! Stan lands flat. ④

Stop and Think

④ Why do you think Stan and Pam fall?

I think they fall because _____

_____

Gramps finds Pam. Gramps finds
Stan. They are so glad! They stamp. They
clap. They clap and clap! **5**

Stop and Think

5 How do the characters feel now? Underline the
words in the story that tell you.

The characters feel _____

_____

"Guess what we have!" says Pam.
But they cannot find them. Everything is
covered. What can they do now?

"Come with me," says Gramps.
"Guess what WE have!" **6**

Stop and Think

6 Where are the acorns?

The acorns are _____

_____

Pam and Stan cannot guess.
"It is in my hand," says Gram.
Stan claps. Pam claps. They like it! **7**

Stop and Think

7 What kind of grandparents are Gram and Gramps?

Gram and Gramps are _____

_____

Think Critically

1. How would you describe Stan and Pam? How would you describe Gram and Gramps? Copy the chart, and fill it in. **CHARACTERS**

Stan and Pam	Gram and Gramps

2. The story takes place in the woods on a fall day. Why is this place important to the story? **PLOT**

This place is important because _____

_____

3. What do you learn about sharing from this story? **AUTHOR'S PURPOSE**

I learn that _____

_____

children

different

ears

finally

hundred

short

Words to Know

Write the word that completes each sentence. The first one has been done for you.

1. There are no kids to be Kim's pal.

There are no _____**children**_____ here.

So Dad will find a pal for Kim.

2. There are a _____ of

them. That is a lot!

3. This one is not like that one. It is

_____ .

4. Look at the _____ one.

It is so little!

5. This rabbit has big _____ .

6. Kim will _____ get a pal.

What will she get?

Write the answer to this question.
Use a complete sentence.

7. What are ears for?

_____

_____

A Pal for Kim

by Anne Riccio

illustrated by Darcia LaBrosse

"Are you sad, Kim?" said Dad.
"No, but there are no children!" **1**

Stop and Think

1 Why does Dad think Kim is sad?

Dad thinks Kim is sad because _____

_____

"I have a plan, Kim. Come on.
We will find a pal for you." **2**

Stop and Think

2 Why does Dad want to help Kim find a pal?

Dad wants to help Kim find a pal so _____

_____

"Look at all of them, Kim," said Dad. "There are a hundred of them. See them swim? You could pick one."

"No. They are not for me, Dad." **3**

Stop and Think

3 Why do you think Kim does not want a fish?

I think Kim does not want a fish because _____

_____

"Look, Kim. See the one on the
swing? It's singing. Will you pick that one?
Or will you pick a different one?"

"No. They are not for me, Dad." **4**

Stop and Think

4 Where do you think Kim and her dad will go next?

I think Kim and her dad will go to _____

_____

© Harcourt

35

"Look, Kim. I like the short one. Do you like it? Will you pick it?"

"No. It's not for me. It isn't the one. Come on, Dad." **5**

Stop and Think

5 Do you think Kim should have picked the dog? Explain your answer.

I think Kim _____

_____

"Look, Kim. It's a rabbit. Look at its big ears! This rabbit likes you!"

"A rabbit is not for me, Dad. It isn't the one. Come on." **6**

Stop and Think

6 How would you feel if you were Kim?

If I were Kim, I would feel _____

_____

"Look what I have, Kim!" Miss Ling said. "It's a gift for you."

"Look, Dad. It's a cat! It licks my hand. It can sit with me. This cat is for me. Finally, this is the one! It will be my pal!" **7**

Stop and Think

7 Why do you think Kim picks a cat for a pet?

I think Kim picks a cat because_____

_____

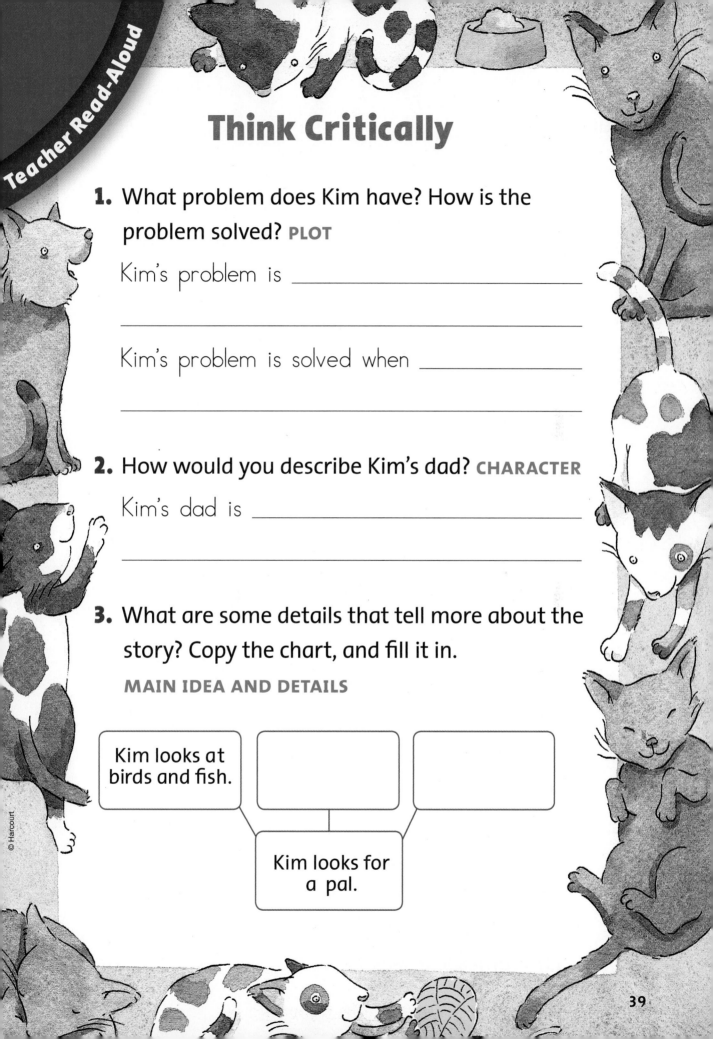

Think Critically

1. What problem does Kim have? How is the problem solved? PLOT

Kim's problem is _____

_____

Kim's problem is solved when _____

_____

2. How would you describe Kim's dad? CHARACTER

Kim's dad is _____

_____

3. What are some details that tell more about the story? Copy the chart, and fill it in.

MAIN IDEA AND DETAILS

| Kim looks at birds and fish. | | |

Kim looks for a pal.

bicycle

exercise

sometimes

special

sugar

Words to Know

Read the selection and think about the meanings of the words in dark type.

Gus

Ben

Gus is a big dog. Ben is not. Ben is as big as a bag of **sugar.**

Lin's dog is Spot. Lin is on her **bicycle.** Spot runs with her. They get a lot of **exercise.**

Pam's dog is Roz. Roz is a **special** dog. Pam can't see. Roz sees for her. **Sometimes** Roz sees when to stop. Sometimes she sees when to go.

Write the word that completes each sentence. The first one has been done for you.

1. Ben is as big as a bag of _____**sugar**_____.

2. Roz has a _____ job. She

sees for Pam.

3. _____ Roz sees when to go.

4. Lin and Spot get a lot

of _____.

5. Lin is on her _____.

Dogs for All

by Christy Yi

illustrated by Johanna Westerman

Do you see the dogs? There is Max. There is Sam. There is Jinx. They are big dogs. They can sit. They can stand. They can dig. ➊

Stop and Think

➊ What do you know about dogs so far?

I know that dogs _____

_____

 Look at the dogs. See Babs. See Fin. See Bon Bon. They are not big. One is as big as a bag of sugar. One is as big as a cat. They can sit in a box or sit on you. **2**

Stop and Think

2 How are Babs, Fin, and Bon Bon alike?

Here is how they are alike: _____

_____

This is Lin. This is her dog Spot. Lin is on her bicycle. Spot runs with her. They get a lot of exercise. ③

Stop and Think

③ What are some other things Lin and Spot might do together?

Lin and Spot might _____

_____

 Some dogs look and find. See Bob. See his dog Oz. They have a big job. They find lost ones. Two are lost now. Bob and Oz have to find them. They look all over. Look! They find them all. **4**

Stop and Think

4 What will the author tell you next about dogs?

I think the author will tell how dogs _____

_____

 See Pam. See her dog Roz. Roz is a special dog. Pam can't see. Roz sees for her. Roz sees when to stop. She sees when to go. Look there! Now they can go. **5**

Stop and Think

5 What are some things Roz might help Pam do?

Roz might help Pam _____

_____

 See Liz and her dog Dot. Dot is a special dog. Liz and Dot visit. Sometimes Dot sits on Ana. Sometimes she licks Tom's hand. Tom and Ana like this dog. They are not sad now. They are glad when Dot comes. **6**

Stop and Think

6 How do dogs help people?

Dogs help people when they _____

_____

Look at the dogs. Dogs for you. Dogs for me. Dogs for all. Do you like dogs? Do you have a dog?

Or do you like cats? **7**

Stop and Think

7 Do you like dogs or cats better? Circle your choice. Then explain it.

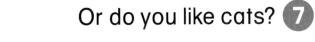

I like dogs/cats better because _____

_____

Think Critically

1. Think about how dogs help us. Copy the chart, and fill it in. **MAIN IDEA AND DETAILS**

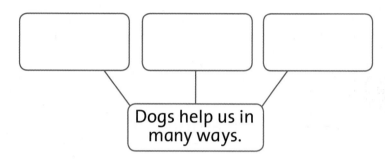

Dogs help us in many ways.

2. How are working dogs different from pet dogs? **MAKE COMPARISONS**

Here's how they are different: _____

_____

_____

3. Why do you think the author tells you about working dogs? **AUTHOR'S PURPOSE**

I think the author tells me about working dogs

because _____

_____

Words to Know

Write the word that best completes each sentence. The first one has been done for you.

1. We are at the ball park. The stands are

_____**already**_____ packed.

different   special   already

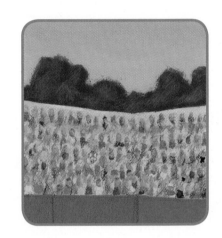

2. There are lots of kids!

A _____ fans have come.

eight   hundred   short

3. I see bats and balls. Do we have

_____ ?

sugar   bicycles   everything

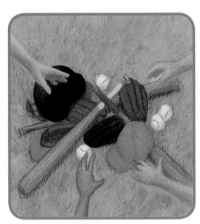

4. I see mitts and caps. I

_____ we do!

guess   exercise   covered

5. We sit and sit. Then we

_____ see a hit!

hundred   through   finally

6. Look at the ball go! It may pass

_____ those two.

through   sometimes   already

7. The ball went over the wall! That's

so _____ to see!

short   special   sometimes

8. Now they have _____ hits.

already   eight   ears

9. Kim is fast. She wants to

_____ it.

prove   special   police

10. She may hit the ball. But

_____ she can't.

sugar   through   sometimes

We All Win!

by Sandra Widener
illustrated by Donald Wu

Cast of Characters

Max Hall	Sam Call	Lin Span
Pat Small	Kit Wal	Tip Ross
Fans		

Max: I guess we have everything. ❶

Stop and Think

❶ What do you think this play will be about?

I think the play will be about _____

_____

Lin: I see bats and balls.

Sam: I see mitts and caps.

Pat: There are a lot of kids!

Tip: A hundred have come. The stands are already packed.

Lin: This is so special.

Max: They all want to see a hit!

Sam: Finally, let's see who is up. **2**

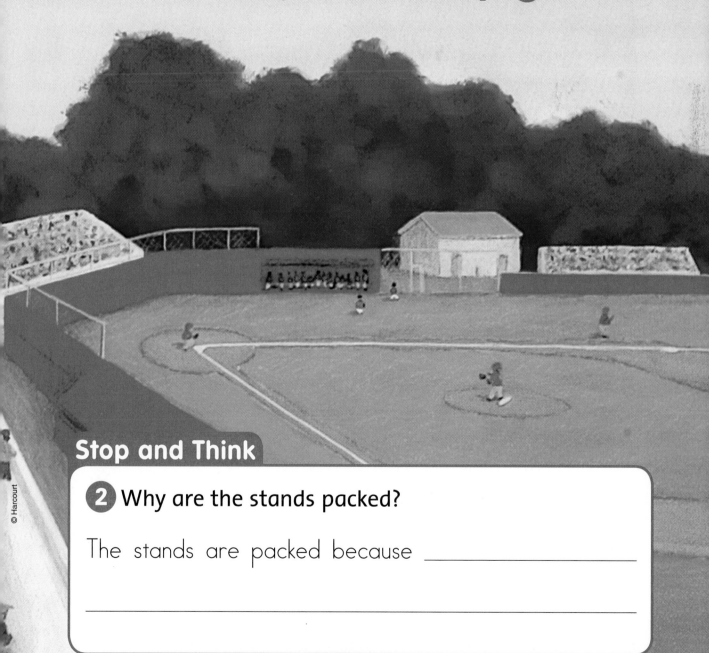

Stop and Think

2 Why are the stands packed?

The stands are packed because _____

_____

Max: Tim takes a swing and hits!
Lin: Will it pass through those two?
Tip: No! The ball is over the wall! ③

Stop and Think

③ How do you think Tim feels when he hits a home run?

I think Tim feels _____

_____

Pat: What a hit!

Lin: Look at that ball go!

Fans: That is what we want to see! **4**

Stop and Think

4 What has happened in the play so far?

So far in the play, _____

_____

Tip: Who is the tall one at bat?

Kit: That's Kim. She is fast.

Kit: But will she prove it?

Sam: No! Sometimes it's a bad ball!

That one was bad.

Fans: She walks! **5**

Stop and Think

5 How is Kim's turn at bat different from Tim's turn?

Kim's turn at bat is different because _____

_____

Lin: Now it's eight to eight.

Kit: Rod is up. He lifts his bat.

Tip: He swings. And it's a hit!

Lin: But look! That kid got the ball.

Max: So that is an out.

Stop and Think

6 What happens when Rod hits?

When Rod hits, _____

_____

Lin: When will this be over?

Tip: And who will win?

Fans: We like it when it's fun like this. When it's like this, we all win!

Stop and Think

7 In what way do fans win when the game is like this one?

Fans win because _____

_____

58

Think Critically

1. **Why does Rod make an out?** CAUSE AND EFFECT

Rod makes an out because _____

_____

_____

2. **What is this story mainly about?** MAIN IDEA
AND DETAILS

This story is mainly about _____

_____

3. **Did the author write this play to teach you
about baseball or to give you something fun to
read? How do you know?** AUTHOR'S PURPOSE

The author wrote this play _____

_____

_____

brother

caught

cheer

learn

lose

straight

Words to Know

Read the selection and think about the meanings of the words in dark type.

Mia Hamm kicked the ball. She kicked it to her **brother**, Garrett. Mia wanted to **learn.** Garrett helped her.

Mia **caught** the ball in her hands. "No, Mia!" Garrett said. "You can't do that!" Then Mia kicked the ball **straight.** She kicked it into the net.

Mia's dad clapped. He liked to **cheer** for her. Mia didn't like to **lose.** She wanted to win!

Write the word that completes each sentence. The first one has been done for you.

1. Garrett is Mia's ___**brother**___ .

2. Mia ___Eaught___ the ball in her hands.

3. Mia wanted to ___Laerh___ to kick.

4. Mia wanted to win. She didn't like to ___Lose___ .

5. Mia's dad liked to ___cheer___ for her.

6. Mia kicked the ball ___Shraight___ into the net.

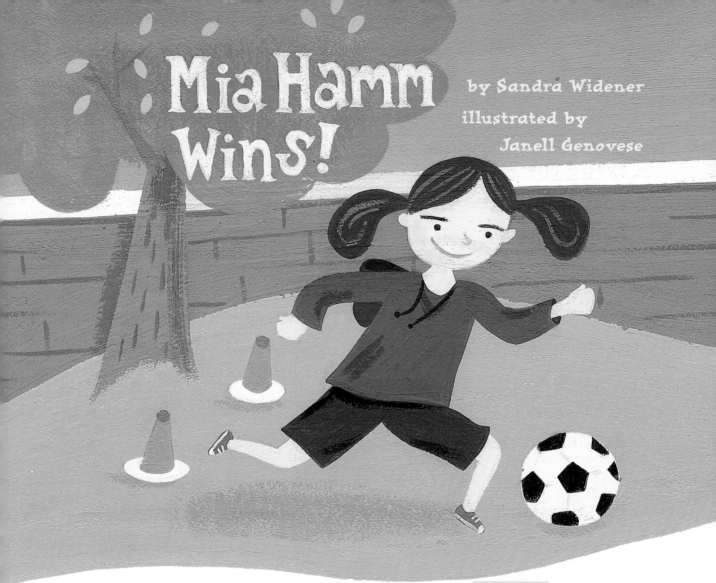

Mia Hamm Wins!

by Sandra Widener

illustrated by
Janell Genovese

Mia Hamm watched her brother,
Garrett. Garrett liked to play ball. Mia
wanted to learn. So Garrett let Mia kick
the ball with him. He helped Mia learn
how to play. **1**

Stop and Think

1 How does Garrett help Mia learn to play soccer?

Garrett helps Mia learn to play soccer by _Mia_
kicking the ball with
him

Mia caught the ball in her hands. "No hands, Mia!" her brother yelled. Could she learn this?

"I can do it, Garrett," Mia said. She kept kicking. She kept at it. ❷

Stop and Think

❷ **What happens in the beginning of this story?**

At the beginning of this story, _Mia caught the ball with her hands._

Mia ran fast. Garrett passed the ball to her. She kicked the ball straight. She sent the ball into the net. Mia began to win a lot! ③

Stop and Think

③ What is your favorite sport or hobby? Why do you like it?

My favorite sport or hobby is *my favorit hobby is video games because they are fun*

Mia's dad helped Mia play and win. Her dad would cheer her on. She won a lot. Mia didn't like to lose. She wanted to be the best. 4

Stop and Think

4 **What do you know about Mia so far?**

I know Mia _wanted it to be the best_

Next, some men asked Mia to play for the United States. It was for the 1996 Olympic Games. "You are one of the best," they said. "Will you play?"

"Yes!" Mia yelled. "I'll go!" **5**

Stop and Think

5 What are some Olympic sports?

Some Olympic sports are _Difficlet_

66

Mia went to play for the United States. Her team passed and kicked the ball. They sent the ball into the net.

Now they were set for the games. They would see who was the best. **6**

Stop and Think

6 **What do you think Mia will do at the Olympics?**

I think Mia will _try her best to win._

The United States went to the games to play. They kicked well. They ran fast. They played well. At last, they won! Mia was so glad!

The United States won the gold medal. With Mia's help, they were the best! **7**

Stop and Think

7 Why do you think the team won the medal?

I think the team won the medal because *They worked as a team*

Think Critically

1. How does the selection end? Copy the chart, and fill it in. **PLOT**

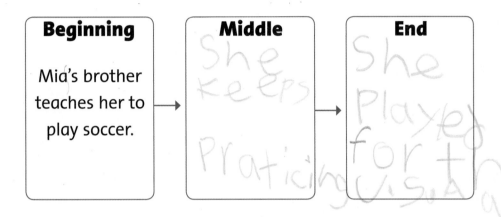

Beginning	Middle	End
Mia's brother teaches her to play soccer.	She keeps praticing	She played for the U.S.A and

woh

2. What happens because Mia practices very hard? **CAUSE AND EFFECT**

Mia practices very hard, so she _____ wen at the Olympics _____

3. What do you think the author wants you to learn from this biography? **AUTHOR'S PURPOSE**

I think the author wants me to learn _about wining and loseing and trying your best_

coming

curve

idea

knee

laughed

million

world

Words to Know

Read the story and think about the meanings of the words in dark type.

I liked softball. But I could not hit. I had missed a **million** balls.

"See my **knee**?" Dad said. "It's bent. Stand like me."

It was a good **idea.** I bent my knee. Then the ball was **coming.** I still missed!

"When I was little, I was not the best in the **world.**" Dad **laughed** as he said this.

Then he said, "Now, this ball will make a **curve.**" Can I hit a ball like that?

© Harcourt

Write the word that completes each sentence. The first one has been done for you.

1. Dad had a good _____**idea**_____ to help me hit.

2. Dad said to bend my _____ .

3. I had missed a _____ balls.

4. The ball was _____ at me.

5. The next ball will make a _____ .

6. Dad _____ at himself.

7. Dad was not the best in the _____ .

I Can Do It

by Anne Riccio

illustrated by Stacey Schuett

I liked softball. I wished I could hit.
But I could not. I missed. And I missed.
And I missed! That was me. I missed a
million balls. They flashed past me. **1**

Stop and Think

1 What is the problem in the story?

The problem is _____

_____

"You can do it!" Dad wished for the best. "Come on. Let's go to the shed. Let's get a bat and ball." **2**

Stop and Think

2 What do you think the boy and his dad will do next?

I think the boy and his dad will _____

_____

"See my knee?" Dad said. "It's bent. Stand like me."

I did.

"Now look," Dad said. "Look at the ball. It's coming!"

It flashed past. I missed the ball. ③

Stop and Think

③ How does Dad try to help the boy?

Dad tries to help the boy by _____

_____

"I have an idea," said Dad. "Let's stop for a bit." **4**

Stop and Think

4 What is Dad like?

Dad is _____

_____

75

"When I was little, I was not the best in the world. I wished I could hit. I missed a lot of balls." Dad laughed.

I flashed him a look. Dad could not hit? I didn't know this. **5**

Stop and Think

5 Why is the boy surprised that his dad could not always hit the ball?

The boy is surprised because _____

_____

"But I kept at it," he added. "Then I could hit. Now, shall we hit some balls?"

I wished. I missed them all. Maybe I was finished.

Dad kept at it. "Look. This ball will make a curve. You can hit it!"

What came next? I hit the ball! **6**

Stop and Think

6 Dad teaches the boy how to hit the ball at last. What else does he teach him?

Dad teaches the boy _____

_____

Splash!

I dashed over to Dad.

"I can do it! I did do it!"

"Yes, you did!" he said. **7**

Stop and Think

7 How do you think the boy feels now?

I think the boy feels _____

_____

78

Think Critically

1. How does Dad help the boy solve his problem? Copy the chart, and fill it in. **PLOT**

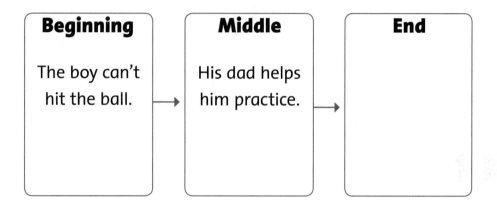

Beginning	**Middle**	**End**
The boy can't hit the ball.	His dad helps him practice.	

2. How are the boy and his dad alike? **MAKE COMPARISONS**

The boy and his dad are both _____

_____

_____

3. What do you learn from this story? **AUTHOR'S PURPOSE**

I learn that _____

_____

accept

ago

clear

fair

half

though

Write the word that completes each sentence. The first one has been done for you.

1. Long _____**ago**_____, Dan and Ron got lost.

2. _____ they were lost, they still went on.

3. They met a big man. It was _____ that he was not like most men.

4. Some men were not _____ as big as him.

© Harcourt

5. The big man wanted Dan and Ron to

_____ a gift.

6. It's _____ to take something

if it is a gift.

**Write the answers to these questions.
Use complete sentences.**

7. The big man will give them a

gift. Is it clear what the gift is?

_____

_____

8. How do you accept a gift?

_____

_____

How We Got Dogs as Pets

by Ann Riccio • illustrated by Cindy Revell

Long ago, Dan and Ron went walking.
Then they got lost.

Dan said, "I'll look for tracks. Tracks
will help us get back home." They found
some small tracks made by an animal.

"Look!" said Ron. "What is that?" **1**

Stop and Think

1 Who is this story about? Where does it take place?

This story is about _____

It takes place in _____

"It looks like a wolf," said Dan. "But it's small." The men didn't know what a dog was.

"Look there!" said Ron. "I see some tracks. But they are BIG!"

"They must be wolf tracks!"

"Stop!" said Dan. "Is that a wolf?" **2**

Stop and Think

2 How do you think Dan and Ron feel now?

I think Dan and Ron feel _____

_____

"Quick! Duck into that tall grass," said Ron. "A wolf must not find us. We are not half as strong!"

But it was a big MAN, not a wolf.

The man was so tall that Dan and Ron had to look up. The big man grinned. "You look lost." **3**

Stop and Think

3 How would you describe the big man?

The big man is _____

_____

© Harcourt

84

"Come with me. You must accept. I can help you. I come from a land over the hills. I am here to visit this land."

Dan and Ron stepped out. Maybe the man could help.

"Can we ask you? What is that?"

"That is a dog. It will do what I ask." **4**

Stop and Think

4 What does the dog do for the man?

The dog _____

_____

The men went to the tent. But then the big man gasped, "Look! Next to the tent! It's a wolf!"

They all stopped. They didn't know what to do. But it was clear that the dog knew what to do. **5**

Stop and Think

5 What do you think the dog will do next?

I think the dog will _____

_____

The dog jumped and ran at the wolf.
"Look!" yelled Dan. "Though it's big, the wolf runs away! See how fast the dog runs? The dog has helped us."

The men were glad when the dog rushed back. **6**

Stop and Think

6 Why does the wolf run away?

The wolf runs away because _____

_____

© Harcou

The dog jumped up. "Maybe the dog can help you get back," the big man said. "Take it."

"But is that fair? It's your dog."

"I'll miss it. But it's a gift for you."

The dog became their pet. And from then on, dogs have been our pets. **7**

Stop and Think

7 Do you think this story is true? Explain your answer.

I think this story _____

_____

© Harcourt

Think Critically

1. In the beginning of the story, Ron and Dan are lost. How is their problem solved? Copy the chart, and fill it in. **PLOT**

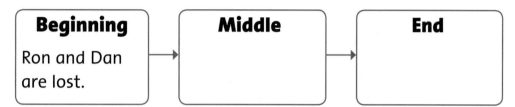

| **Beginning** | **Middle** | **End** |
| Ron and Dan are lost. | | |

2. How are dogs and wolves alike? How are they different? **COMPARE AND CONTRAST**

Here's how they are alike: _____

_____

_____

Here's how they are different: _____

_____

_____

3. Why do you think the author wrote this tale? **AUTHOR'S PURPOSE**

I think the author wrote this tale _____

_____

believe

brought

early

enough

impossible

quite

understand

Words to Know

Read the story and think about the meanings of the words in dark type.

It was **early.** The sun had just come up. "I am **quite** sick of this," said Red. "I will not get Ma and Pa up."

"That is **impossible!**" said Pig. "You must get them up!"

Hen did not **understand.** "But who will get them up?" said Hen.

"I do not **believe** you," said Duck. Duck **brought** a clock. "You will get them up."

"No, I have had **enough,**" said Red. "I do not like this job!"

Write the word that completes each sentence. The first one has been done for you.

1. Red does not like his job. He has had

_____**enough**_____ of it.

2. Red was _____ sick of

getting them up.

3. The sun was up. It was

_____ .

4. Duck did not _____ Red.

5. "That is _____!" said Pig.

Red must get them up.

6. Hen did not _____. "Who

will get them up?" she said.

7. Duck _____ a clock to Red.

Get Up!
Get Up!

by **Anne Riccio** illustrated by **Jannie Ho**

The sun was up. The animals were up.
But Ma and Pa were not up.

"What is this?" asked Hen. "What is going on?"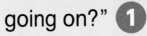

Stop and Think

1 When and where does this story take place?

This story takes place _____

_____

"It's early," said Red. "I want to rest. They can rest as well."

The animals thought that this was bad. "But you must get them up!" said Pig.

"Thanks," said Red. "But I do not want this job. I have had enough."

Stop and Think

2 What is Red's job?

Red's job is _____

_____

At last, Pa got up. "What?" yelled Pa. "Ten o'clock! That can't be! That's impossible!"

Ma got up. "I do not believe this. What happened?"

"Let's go find out," said Pa. ③

Stop and Think

③ Why is Red's job important?

Red's job is important because _____

_____

"What happened?" Pa asked.

"I do not like getting up early," said Red.

"I do not understand. It's your job. How will Ma and I get up?"

"You can get up when you want. I want to rest." **4**

Stop and Think

4 If you were Red, would you like to get up so early? Explain your answer.

If I were Red, I would _____

_____

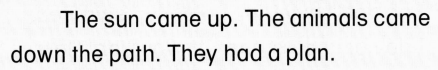

The sun came up. The animals came down the path. They had a plan.

"Did you bring pots?" asked Hen. "Do you have pans?"

"Yes," said Duck. "We brought them." **5**

Stop and Think

5 What do you think the animals will do next?

I think the animals will _____

_____

© Harcourt

Pans clapped. Pots banged.

"Get up. Get up!" they all yelled.

Pa jumped out of bed. "What is this?

That's quite enough! I'm up. I'm up!"

"What happened to Red?" asked Ma.

"Red can do this best." **6**

Stop and Think

6 Who would you choose to wake you up—Red or the animals with their pots and pans? Tell why.

I would choose _____

_____

"Red, we want to get up," said Pa.
"But we do not want to get up like that."

"What can we do?" asked Ma. "What
do you want, Red?"

"Let me rest some," said Red. "This is
when I want to rest. Then, I'll get you up."

"We can do that," said Pa. "Now, let's
all get some rest!" **7**

Stop and Think

7 Why do you think the author wrote this story?

The author wrote this story _____

_____

Think Critically

1. How is the problem in the story solved?
Copy the chart, and fill it in. **PLOT**

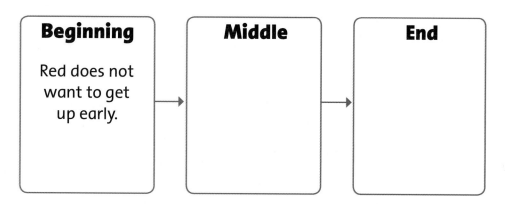

Beginning	Middle	End
Red does not want to get up early.		

2. How would you describe Red? **CHARACTER**

I think Red is _____

_____

3. Why do you think the animals helped Red?
MAKE INFERENCES

I think the animals helped Red because

_____

_____

Words to Know

Write the word that best completes each sentence. The first one has been done for you.

1. The class will be _____**coming**_____ to visit the park.

   caught coming enough

2. Martha has an _____ . She will let them

   idea   knee   world

help in the garden.

3. The students will _____ to plant things.

   learn   lose   caught

4. _____ it is hard, the students still help.

   Clear   Enough   Though

5. They give the plants just

_____ water. Not too much!

enough   clear   ago

6. Bart tells them, "Long _____ ,

ago   clear   enough

there was no park."

7. "We dug a pond. Then we

_____ fish for it."

learned   caught   lose

8. It is a good park. The kids do not

want to _____ it.

understand   lose   learn

9. It's _____ that they want

ago   coming   clear

to help the park.

10. Now they _____ how

lose   caught   understand

they can help.

A Visit to the Park

by Steve Davis

illustrated by Jared Lee

Characters

Narrator

Bart

Carl

Martha

Students

Narrator: The class has come for a visit. They have come to see the park.

Students: Mmmmm! The park smells so fresh. **1**

Stop and Think

1 Why do you think the park smells fresh?

The park smells fresh because _____

_____

Bart: I smell grass.

Carl: I smell the plants in the gardens.

Martha: I smell . . . the barn!

Students: She smells the barn?

Martha: Yes! It is a part of this park. **2**

Stop and Think

2 What does the class smell? Underline the words that tell you.

The class smells _____

_____

Bart: Do you want to know more about the park?

Students: Yes, we do!

Martha: I have an idea. We can help you learn to garden.

Carl: Then you will understand how you can help the park.

Students: Yes! We want to help! **3**

Stop and Think

3 How do you think the children feel about learning to garden?

I think the children feel _____

_____

Bart: We have to make a garden.

Carl: We dig a spot for the plants. We put the plants in. Then we water them.

Martha: Give the plants just enough water. Not too much!

Students: This is hard! But it's fun! **4**

Stop and Think

4 What do the gardeners do to make a garden?

To make a garden, the gardeners _____

_____

Bart: Long ago, there was no farm in this spot. There was no garden. There was no park at all!

Carl: We made the paths and gardens.

Bart: And we dug a pond. Then, we caught fish for the pond. **5**

Stop and Think

5 What did the gardeners do to make the park?

To make the park, the gardeners _____

_____

Martha: Though it was hard, we all did our part.

Bart: And now *you* can do your part.

Students: What can we do? Tell us!

Carl: It's clear you want to help the park. These are the things you can do. **6**

Stop and Think

6 What do you think the gardeners will tell the children?

I think the gardeners will tell them to _____

_____

Martha: Pick up things that do not belong here.

Carl: Do not harm the plants.

Bart: Tell your pals how to help. If we all take care of a park, then with your help, we will not lose the park.

Narrator: The kids have to go now. But they will be coming back!

Students: Thanks for letting us visit! We will be back to do our part! **7**

Stop and Think

7 What will happen if we all take care of a park?

If we all take care of a park, then _____

_____

© Harcourt

Think Critically

1. How do you think the land looked before the gardeners did their work? **COMPARE AND CONTRAST**

Before, the land looked _____

_____

_____

2. How do you think Bart, Carl, and Martha feel about the park? Why? **CHARACTERS**

I think they feel _____

_____

_____

3. What do you think the author wants you to learn from this play? **AUTHOR'S PURPOSE**

I think the author wants me to learn that

_____

_____

Words to Know

bought

draw

especially

minute

picture

question

sure

worry

Write the word that completes each sentence. The first one has been done for you.

1. Mom _____**bought**_____ me a sketch pad. It didn't cost much.

2. I will _____ in my sketch pad. It will be fun.

3. I will make a _____ in my sketch pad.

4. I will make one _____ for my pal Marta.

5. But I am not _____

where I put my sketch pad.

6. I do not _____ about it

much. I will find it.

7. In just a _____, I find my

art things.

8. Now I have a _____. What

will I draw for Marta?

A Garden *for* Marta

by Anne Riccio ⋯ illustrated by Marit Menzin

This is Marta. She has a garden. It's big! It has carrots, which I like. It has spinach, which I do not like. Not at all. **1**

Stop and Think

1 What does Marta grow in her garden?

In her garden, Marta grows _____

_____

_____

This fall, Marta fell. Now she can't walk, which is very sad. She can't pick spinach, which is not so sad. I want to help Marta. I want to make her glad. But what can I do? I have to sit and think about it. ❷

Stop and Think

❷ **What do you know about Marta so far?**

I know that Marta _____

_____

_____

Mom comes in.

"I think I'll make a picture," I tell her. "A picture for Marta."

"Where is your sketch pad?" she asks. "The one I bought you."

"I'm not sure," I tell her. "But do not worry. I'll find it." **3**

Stop and Think

3 What have you done to help someone feel better?

To help someone feel better, I _____

_____

_____

I find my art things. Now I have a new question. What will I draw?

I think. I think again. I look all around. I think of what Marta would like. Then it comes to me. I know just what to draw. **4**

Stop and Think

4 What do you think the girl will draw?

I think the girl will draw _____

_____

_____

In a minute, I am sketching. I sketch and sketch. I go on sketching. Mom tells me my hand will fall off! **5**

Stop and Think

5 Find the sentence "Mom tells me my hand will fall off!" What does Mom really mean?

Mom really means that _____

_____

At last, I finish. I go up to Marta. I hand her my picture.

"This is especially for you," I tell her.

She looks at it. I watch her. Will she like it?

She grins. Then she hugs me. Yes, I think she likes it. **6**

Stop and Think

6 Why do you think Marta likes the drawing?

I think that _____

_____

_____

"This is the best garden," Marta tells me.
"Thank you so much! It makes me happy."

"Marta, do you know what will make me happy?" I ask her. "Planting spinach next spring with you!" **7**

Stop and Think

7 What do you learn from this story?

I learn that _____

_____

_____

Think Critically

1. How does the girl make Marta feel better? Copy the chart, and fill it in. **PLOT**

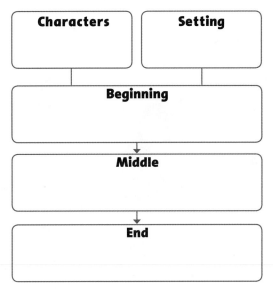

2. How would you describe the girl? **CHARACTER**

The girl is _____

_____

_____

3. Why does the picture make Marta feel better?

   CAUSE AND EFFECT

The picture makes Marta feel better because

_____

_____

board

cook

enjoy

expensive

favorite

imagine

popular

year

Read the selection and think about the meanings of the words in dark type.

What do you **enjoy**? Some of us **cook.** Some of us play games.

You can play some games on a **board.** Some of them are **expensive.** Many do not cost a lot. Mancala is one **popular** game. Many children like to play it.

What if you could play just one thing for a **year**? **Imagine** that. Which **favorite** game would you pick?

© Harcourt

Write the word that completes each sentence.
The first one has been done for you.

1. Some children like to _____ **cook** _____ snacks.

2. Games are fun. Children

_____ playing them.

3. Many children like Mancala. It's a

_____ game.

4. Some games are played on a _____ .

5. A game that costs a lot is _____ .

6. Your _____ game is the one you

like the most.

7. Some games you can play all

_____ long.

8. Can you _____ doing that?

Think about it.

How We Play

by **Anne Riccio**
illustrated by **Ann Boyajian**

What do you do for fun? Do you swim at the shore? Do you fish? Do you like to help your mom and dad cook? What is your favorite game to play? What is your favorite sport? You do not have to be bored. Not when there is so much to do! **1**

Stop and Think

1 What do you do for fun?

For fun, I like to _____

_____

_____

Imagine you are on a trip. You go far, far away. But all over, you see children play. They run. They hit a ball and catch it. All of them have fun. Just like you! ②

Stop and Think

② How do you think all children have fun?

I think all children _____

_____

_____

Do you know this sport? Lots of us enjoy it. We hit the ball across a court. We watch the ball go back and forth.

Far away, some children play cricket. It's like softball. You hit a ball and score runs. **3**

Stop and Think

3 What games do children play in the United States and other countries?

Children play _____

_____

Mancala is popular in Kenya. Children here play it, too. You can get this board game at a store. But it's less expensive to make one. Use an egg carton, and play with small rocks.

One, two, three. Put a rock in a new spot. Think of a plan, and you can win. Find out how to play Mancala. You'll have fun. **4**

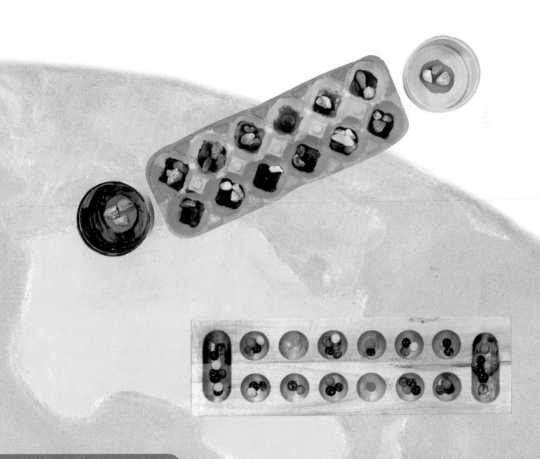

Stop and Think

4 Why do children like to play Mancala?

Children like to play Mancala because _____

_____

_____

125

See the tops? Four tops spin. Can you spin a top? Can you spin four? Can you spin more? **5**

Stop and Think

5 What does the author want you to learn from this selection?

The author wants me to learn _____

_____

In Mexico, this boy kicks the ball. He runs. He scores!

Many children watch this sport. Many of them play it. Small children play. Big ones play, too. It's a sport many like a lot. **6**

Stop and Think

6 Why do so many people like soccer?

Many people like soccer because _____

_____

_____

© Harcourt

Children play all **year**. They have fun. They like to do many things.

Children can play with things they find. They play with small rocks. They use a stick for a bat. They catch and kick. They jump and run. They find things to do, just like you. **7**

Stop and Think

7 The author describes many games. Which is your favorite game? Why?

My favorite game is _____

_____

Think Critically

1. Why is it less expensive to make a Mancala game than to buy one? **CAUSE AND EFFECT**

It's less expensive because _____

_____

_____

2. What games do you play? What games do children play in other parts of the world? Copy the chart, and fill it in. **COMPARE AND CONTRAST**

Games I Play	Games Children Play Around the World

3. What is this article mostly about? **MAIN IDEA AND DETAILS**

This article is mostly about _____

_____

_____

| above |
| shoes |
| tough |
| wash |
| wear |
| woman |
| young |

Words to Know

Write the word that completes each sentence. The first one has been done for you.

1. Bert will _____**wash**_____ up and

dress for class.

2. Bert will _____ a purple

shirt.

3. Bert will put on his _____ .

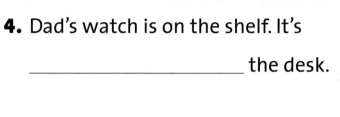

4. Dad's watch is on the shelf. It's

_____ the desk.

5. Dad got this watch when he was

_____ .

6. It would be _____ to

find another one like it.

7. Bert will let a _____ see

the watch.

Write the answers to these questions.
Use complete sentences.

8. What shirt will Bert wear?

_____

_____

9. What will Bert let the woman do?

_____

_____

The Lost Watch

by Anne Riccio

illustrated by Teresa Flavin

"Dad, it's my turn to talk in class. Can I take your pocket watch?"

"It's an old watch, Bert. It would be tough to find another like it. You must take care of it."

"I'd never let anything happen to it, Dad."

"OK. It'll be in good hands," said Dad.

"Thanks, Dad." **1**

Stop and Think

1 What do you know about the story so far?

I know _____

_____

_____

© Harcourt

The next morning, Bert got up. He went to wash up. What shirt did he want to wear? He would wear the purple one. Bert put on his pants and shoes.

Bert walked past his father's desk. He got the watch from the shelf above the desk. Bert put it in his pocket. **2**

Stop and Think

2 How do you think Bert feels as he gets ready for school? Why?

I think Bert feels _____

_____

It was Bert's turn to talk. He held up the watch for the class to see.

"This is my dad's watch," he said. "He got it from his father when he was young."

"Thank you, Bert," said Miss Dunn.

"Can we see?" asked the other children.

Bert was all set to say no. But he passed around the watch. He felt good. **3**

Stop and Think

3 Do you think it was a good idea to pass around the watch? Explain your answer.

I think _____

_____

"Mom? Dad? I'm back!" yelled Bert. Mom yelled back from the kitchen.

Bert went to put the watch back. He looked in all of his pockets. It was not there. He looked all over. He could not find his father's watch.

"I'd better get that watch back." **4**

Stop and Think

4 **What is the problem in the story?**

The problem is _____

_____

_____

At dinner, Bert's parents wondered how his talk went.

"How was it?" asked his father.

Bert gulped. What could he say? He started to talk. But then he saw a woman on the front porch. His sister went to see who it was.

"Bert, it's for you. I think it's Miss Dunn." **5**

Stop and Think

5 Why do you think Miss Dunn came to see Bert?

Miss Dunn came to see Bert because _____

_____

_____

"Bert, I found your father's watch."

"Thanks, Miss Dunn. I was wondering where it was."

"It was on my desk," said Miss Dunn.

"Well, thanks so much. I'd better give it back to my dad now." **6**

Stop and Think

6 **What do you think Bert will do next?**

I think Bert will _____

_____

_____

"That was Miss Dunn," said Bert. "She came over with your watch. I know you trusted me with it. The other kids wanted to see it. So, I passed it around. When I got back home, I couldn't find it."

"I'm glad it's back, Bert. I think it would be best if the watch was kept on my shelf."

"Yes, Dad. That is the best spot for it."

"It's the best spot until it is your watch."

Bert hugged his dad. Then he put the watch back. **7**

Stop and Think

7 Is this story fiction or nonfiction? How do you know?

This story is _____

_____

Think Critically

1. Think about what happens in the story. Copy the chart, and fill it in. **PLOT**

Beginning	Middle	End
Bert shares his dad's watch.	Bert can't find his dad's watch	

2. How does Bert lose his Dad's watch? **CAUSE AND EFFECT**

Bert loses his dad's watch because _____

_____

_____

3. What does this story teach you? **AUTHOR'S PURPOSE**

This story teaches me that _____

_____

_____

Words to Know

care

father

interesting

sweat

thumb

touch

Read the selection and think about the meanings of the words in dark type.

All cats are **interesting.** Some are big. Some are little. When it's hot out, you can see your **sweat.** But cats do not have sweat.

There are not many big cats left. Talk to those who take **care** of them. They can tell you about them. Talk to your mother or **father,** too.

But remember: do not **touch** a big cat. Never put a finger or **thumb** where a big cat can get it!

© Harcourt

Write the word that completes each sentence.
The first one has been done for you.

1. Never put a _____**thumb**_____

where a big cat can get it.

2. Do not _____ a big cat.

It can hurt you.

3. All cats are _____ . It's

fun to learn about them.

4. Your mother or _____

may tell you about cats.

5. It may get hot. But you will not see

_____ on a cat.

6. You can talk to those who take

_____ of cats.

CATS

by Anne Riccio

illustrated by Lou Francher and Steve Johnson

Do you like cats? What about big cats? How about fast cats? What about cats that purr? How about cats that growl?

There are thirty-six different sorts of cats. All of them are interesting. Some you can see in your yard. **1**

Stop and Think

1 What do you already know about cats?

I know that cats are _____

_____

_____

Cats have whiskers. Cats use them to touch things. Whiskers help cats get around in the dark.

Cats have fur. Their fur can be all one color. Or it can be many colors. A cat's fur is thick. But when it's hot, cats find a spot that is not. They have to. They do not have sweat like we do. **2**

Stop and Think

2 Is this selection fiction or nonfiction? How do you know?

This selection is _____

_____

This cat hunts in the dark. Its dark fur makes it hard to see. It prowls without a sound.

It hunts in the water, too. How? It swims! It can catch fish and turtles. It picks them right out of the water. **3**

JAGUAR

© Harcourt

Stop and Think

3 What do you know about jaguars now? Underline the words that tell you.

I know that jaguars _____

_____

This cat hunts in the dark, too. It looks for small animals on the ground. When it sees one, down it runs. Then the cat jumps and catches it. **4**

MARGAY

Stop and Think

4 What kinds of animals do you think this cat might hunt?

This cat might hunt _____

_____

This cat lives in the forest. It has tan fur with black spots. Its spots help the cat blend in.

This cat runs fast. It swims, too. It hunts birds and other animals. It catches fish and frogs in the water. 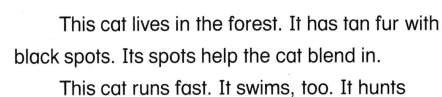 **5**

LEOPARD

Stop and Think

5 The author tells you that a leopard's spots help it "blend in." How does this help it?

The leopard's spots help it because _____

_____

Some people want to hurt these big cats.
They want their fur. Now, there are not so many
big cats left.

Stop and Think

6 What do you think will happen if some people keep
hurting these big cats?

I think that _____

_____

How can you help? Talk to your mother or your father. Talk to those who take care of big cats. Find out all about big cats. Ask what you can do to help.

But remember: Look, but do not touch. Be careful. Never put a finger or a thumb where a big cat can get it! **7**

LIONS →
TIGERS ←
PUMAS ←

Stop and Think

7 What are some things you can do to help big cats?

These are some things I can do to help big cats:

_____

_____

© Harcourt

Think Critically

1. What do you learn about cats? Copy the chart, and fill it in. MAIN IDEA AND DETAILS

| What I Know | What I Want to Know | What I Learned |

2. How are pet cats and big cats the same? How are they different? COMPARE AND CONTRAST

Here are ways they are the same: _____

_____

_____

Here are ways they are different: _____

_____

_____

3. What does the author want you to learn from this selection? AUTHOR'S PURPOSE

The author wants me to learn _____

_____

_____

Words to Know

Write the word that best completes each sentence. The first one has been done for you.

1. Tim wants to know who will come to the picnic

this _____ **year** _____ .

year   minute   question

2. That's the _____ he asks

minute   question   year

his sister.

3. Tim wants to _____ the picnic.

wash   wear   enjoy

4. Shane _____ likes the hot dogs.

imagine   especially   interesting

5. He can't _____ a picnic

wear   imagine   wash

without hot dogs.

6. Gabe says, "My _____ and I will come."

        father   minute   year

7. Gabe will bring an _____

        especially   tough   interesting

game to play.

8. Tim will _____ his hands.

        wear   wash   enjoy

9. He will pick out a shirt to

_____ to the picnic.

wash   imagine   wear

10. In just a _____ , Tim will find

        father   question   minute

out who will be at the picnic.

Write the answers to these questions. Use complete sentences.

11. What does Shane especially enjoy at a picnic? _____

_____

12. What will Tim find out in a minute? _____

_____

The Picnic

by Anne Riccio

illustrated by Beatriz Helen Ramos

Cast of Characters

Narrator	Shane	Kate
Tim	Gabe	Gram
Jane	Kim	Gramps

Narrator: There is a picnic at three o'clock in the Maxwells' yard.

Tim: Jane, who did Mom ask to the picnic?

Jane: I don't know. Maybe she asked someone new. We will find out later. **1**

Stop and Think

1 Why does the author list all the characters?

The author lists all the characters because

_____

_____

Tim: But I would like to know now!

Jane: Why? You will enjoy the picnic no matter who comes. ❷

Stop and Think

❷ **What problem does Tim have?**

Tim's problem is _____

_____

_____

153

Narrator: Tim thinks of who came last year. First, he calls Shane.

Tim: You came to our picnic last year. Did my mom ask you this year? Will you come?

Shane: She didn't ask. But I'll be there! I especially like your hot dogs! **3**

Stop and Think

3 What are some things you can do at a picnic?

At picnics, I _____

_____

_____

Narrator: Next, Tim calls Gabe.

Tim: You came to our picnic last year. Did my mom ask you this year? Will you come?

Gabe: She didn't ask. But my father and I will come! We will bring interesting games. **4**

Stop and Think

4 Is this story real or imaginary? How do you know?

This story is _____

_____

_____

Narrator: Next, Tim calls Kim.

Tim: Kim, I have a question. You came to our picnic last year. Did my mom ask you this year? Will you come?

Kim: No, she didn't ask. But I'll be there! And my mom will be there, too. **5**

Stop and Think

5 Why do Tim's friends all want to come to the picnic?

Tim's friends want to come to the picnic because

_____

_____

Narrator: Last, Tim calls Kate.

Tim: Kate, you came to our picnic last year. Will you come this year?

Kate: I can't imagine not going to your picnic. I'll be there.

Tim: Who did Mom ask? I will find out in a minute.

Jane: Tim, wash your hands and pick out what to wear. ⑥

Stop and Think

⑥ Do you think Tim will enjoy the picnic? Explain your answer.

I think Tim _____

_____

Narrator: It's three o'clock. Shane, Gabe, Kim, and Kate are here. And so are . . .

Tim: Gram and Gramps!

Gram: Tim! Jane! We are here!

Gramps: Is there a picnic here?

Tim: Yes! Jane was right! She said I'd enjoy the picnic. But now I know I'll enjoy it more! **7**

Stop and Think

7 Why did the author write this play?

The author wrote this play _____

_____

_____

Think Critically

1. Who are the special guests at the picnic? PLOT

The special guests are_____

_____

2. How would you describe Tim? CHARACTER

Tim is _____

_____

3. How are Tim and his sister alike? How are they different? COMPARE AND CONTRAST

Here is how they are alike:_____

_____

Here is how they are different: _____

_____

© Harcourt

celebrate

cozy

enchanting

instead

review

thrilled

Vocabulary

Build Robust Vocabulary

Write the Vocabulary Word that completes each sentence. The first one has been done for you.

1. It's wet out. But it's _____cozy_____ at home.

2. Duke and June can't go out. They sit at home _____ .

3. June will make some _____ art. It will be so charming.

4. Mom will look. She will give the art a _____ .

© Harcourt

5. If Mom likes it, June will be _____ .

6. Then they will have fun. They will _____ .

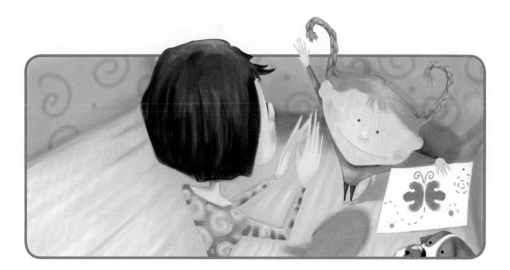

Write the Vocabulary Word that best completes the synonym web.

7.

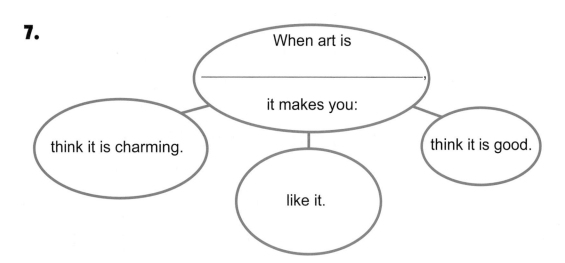

When art is _____, it makes you:

think it is charming.

like it.

think it is good.

The Art Hound

by Sandra Widener
illustrated by Joanne Kollman

Duke and June sit at home. Duke has his nose on June's leg. It's cozy, but they are sad. They want to go out. They want to run around. They want to poke at mole holes. They would play until it's dark. Then Duke can't see his nose. But it's too wet. So June and Duke just sit at home. **1**

Stop and Think

1 Why do Duke and June sit at home?

Duke and June sit at home because _____

_____

_____

Val is June's pal. She comes over to play. "What can we do?"

Mom thinks. "You can make some art."

So they do. Then June and Val take a vote. They will go with Mom. Duke looks very sad. June talks to Duke. "You can't go. Be good." **2**

Stop and Think

2 Why is Duke sad?

Duke is sad because _____

_____

_____

Duke is all alone. He mopes. Then he sniffs. What does he smell?

Duke gets up. He pokes at a pot. Then he tips it. Brown and red go all over.

Duke runs right into it. What a mess! ❸

Stop and Think

❸ **Who are the characters in this story?**

The characters are _____

_____

_____

Then June gets home. She sees the mess. Duke's nose is red. It's brown, too! June is mad at Duke. "This is not cute. And it's not art! What will I do?"

Duke mopes some more. **4**

Stop and Think

4 What do you think June will do?

I think June will _____

_____

_____

June washes up the mess. Then she looks. She sees the spots Duke made. June has a plan. "I can see art. Those spots are not just spots. They can be art instead!"

June gets a tube of black. She makes some marks. **5**

Stop and Think

5 What is June's plan?

June's plan is _____

_____

_____

June pats Duke's nose. Duke is glad. June is not mad. Duke uses his nose some more. He makes a new red spot. June makes more marks. They look like the spots on Duke's fur.

June steps back to give their work a review. She is thrilled. They have made art! **6**

Stop and Think

6 Did the author write this story to make you laugh or to tell you facts? How do you know?

The author wrote this story to _____

_____

June calls to Mom. Now, there are no bad marks. There is just the art. June and Duke made it. Mom is glad. "Enchanting! Let's celebrate!"

Mom claps as Duke and June bow. Then Mom looks at Duke. She wants to know. Why is his nose red? **7**

Stop and Think

7 How do you think June feels when Mom claps?

I think June feels _____

_____

_____

© Harcourt

Think Critically

1. How does Duke make a big mess? **PLOT**

Duke makes a big mess when he _____

_____

_____

2. After Duke makes a mess, what does June do?
CAUSE AND EFFECT

After Duke makes a mess, June _____

_____

_____

3. Think about what happens in the story. Copy the chart, and fill it in. **SEQUENCE**

Beginning	Middle	End

carefree

entertain

except

screeching

sipped

stomped

Vocabulary

Build Robust Vocabulary

Read the story and think about the meanings of the words in dark type.

Ben felt **carefree** as he rested in the shade. He **sipped** his drink. Then Sal played a **screeching** sound. "What is that?" cried Ben.

It was Sal playing her bagpipes.

Then Kate and Sam came up. They each had something to play.

"We are a band!" Sam said. "We can **entertain** our families. We are all here **except** Greg."

Then Greg came. Sam and Greg **stomped** around as they played. Ben felt sad. "I want something to play," he said.

© Harcourt

Write the Vocabulary Word that completes each sentence. The first one has been done for you.

1. Ben felt calm as he rested. He felt

_____**carefree**_____.

2. Sal's bagpipes made a _____ sound.

3. All the players had come _____ Greg.

4. The band will _____ their

families. They will play for them.

5. Ben _____ his drink.

6. Greg and Sam _____ around as

they played.

The Band

by David James

illustrated by Deb Pilutti

What a fine morning it was! Ben sat in the shade and sipped his drink. But before long, he felt tired. Ben tried to rest.

"SQUAAK!" What was that screeching sound? It woke Ben up.

It was Sal. She smiled at Ben.

"It's time to get up and play!" she cried. Then she started to play her bagpipes again. **1**

Stop and Think

1 Where does this story take place?

This story takes place _____

_____

_____

"No!" Ben cried. "Stop!"

"But I like to play!" Sal said.

"I wish I had something to play," said Ben.

Just then Kate arrived. She had some chimes. "Is it time to play?" Kate asked.

"Not yet," Sal said. "We invited Greg and Sam, too. We can't play without them." ❷

Stop and Think

❷ **Why are Sal and Kate waiting for Sam and Greg?**

Sal and Kate are waiting for Sam and Greg

because _____

_____

"I want something to play," Ben said. Then Sam arrived. He had a trumpet. "I do not like being late," he said. "But my bike had a flat. We are all here except Greg." ③

Stop and Think

③ **Why does Ben want something to play?**

Ben wants something to play because _____

_____

_____

© Harcourt

While they sat, Sal tried some sounds.
Kate rang her chimes. Sam began to play
some notes.

"I want something to play," Ben cried.
Then Greg arrived with his clarinet.
"You are just in time!" said Kate.

Stop and Think

4 Why does Ben say he wants something to play over and over again?

Ben says this because _____

_____

Sal, Kate, Sam, and Greg started to play a song. But Ben didn't like it.

"Stop!" he said. "It does not sound quite right. I think I know what is missing. Stay here. I'll be right back." **5**

Stop and Think

5 What do you think Ben is going to do?

I think Ben will _____

_____

_____

Ben went to the other side of the yard. There he found a wide pine log. Its insides had rotted away. He found some sticks beside the log.

"These will do just fine," Ben said.

Ben tied some twine around the log. He grabbed the twine and tugged. Then he dragged the log back to the others. **6**

Stop and Think

6 What kind of person is Ben? Explain your answer.

I think Ben is _____

_____

_____

"Let's strike up the band!" Ben cried.

So Sal piped away on her bagpipes. Kate chimed in. Sam and Greg stomped around as they made their sounds. Ben kept time by hitting the log with the sticks.

Their song sounded just right. They could entertain their families with these sounds now. Ben smiled. He felt carefree. At last he had something to play! **7**

Stop and Think

7 Do you think their families will enjoy the song? Explain.

I think their families _____

_____

Think Critically

1. What happens in the story? Copy the chart, and fill it in. **PLOT**

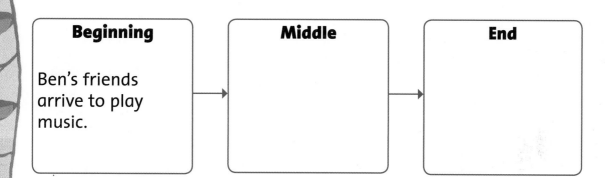

Beginning	Middle	End
Ben's friends arrive to play music.		

2. How does Ben feel at the end of the story? Explain. **CHARACTER**

   Ben feels _____

   _____

3. Did the author write this story to make you smile or to give you facts? How do you know?
   AUTHOR'S PURPOSE

   The author wrote this story _____

   _____

   _____

concentrate

creative

expression

performance

relieved

volume

Vocabulary

Build Robust Vocabulary

Write the Vocabulary Word that completes each sentence. The first one has been done for you.

1. Let's plan a _____ performance _____

   for our families.

2. Let's come up with something good.

   Let's be _____ !

3. Our beat is an _____

   of who we are.

4. The _____ is up. The beat

is fast and loud!

5. We must _____ as we

tap. We want to get it right.

6. We did well! We are so _____ .

**Write the Vocabulary Word that best
completes the synonym web.**

7.

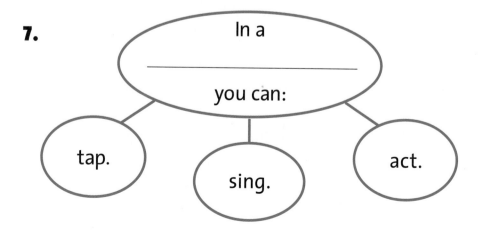

In a
_____
you can:

tap.

sing.

act.

Keep the Beat

by Sandra Widener
illustrated by Allan Eitzen

Hear the beat of that tune? You start to step and leave your seat. Your feet tip-tap. The volume is up. The beat is fast. You can't stop! Up the steps you tap.

You just need to feel that beat.

Stop and Think

1 **What do you think this selection will be about?**

I think this selection will be about _____

_____

_____

The beat we keep is an expression of who we are. Be creative with your beat. You can keep it fast, but you do not have to.

Leap to the beat, or tap your feet on the street. Your beat will feel just right. **2**

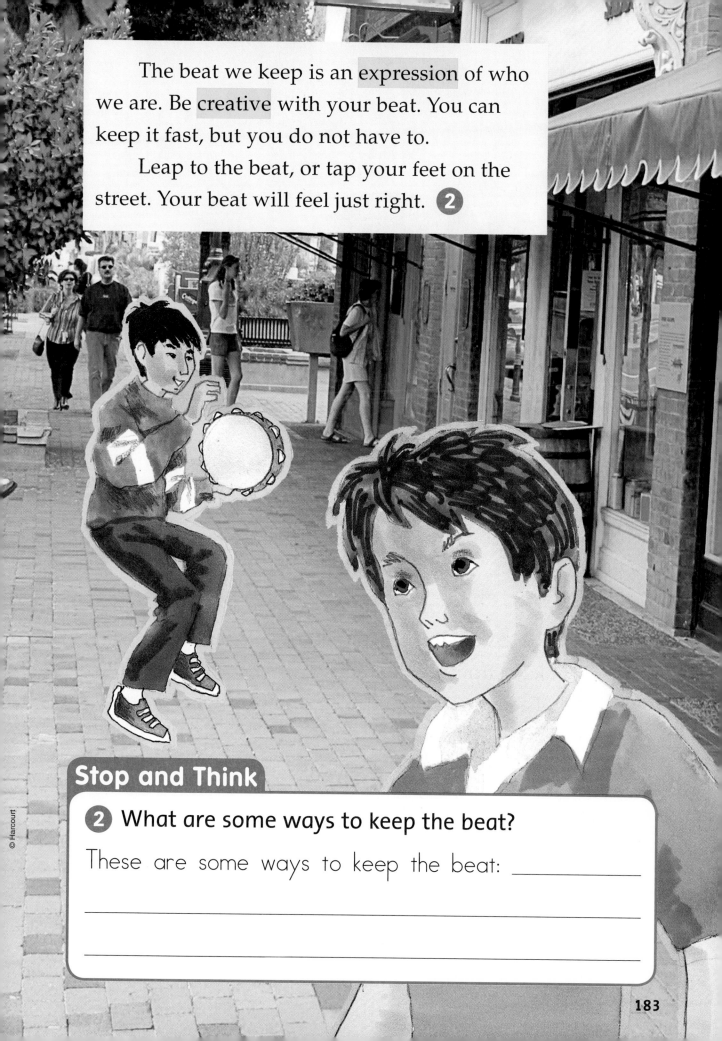

Stop and Think

2 What are some ways to keep the beat?

These are some ways to keep the beat: _____

_____

_____

A tap team is a treat to see. You can't keep from feeling their beat. Their beat is fast! Their feet are loud! You can hear them up and down the street. **3**

Stop and Think

3 What makes a tap team fun to see?

A tap team is fun to see because _____

_____

_____

184

Three Cheers

Keeping a beat to a song can be someone's job. So can leaping. Making notes and leaping are hard work. When you hear someone play well, give three cheers! When you see a good leap, give three more cheers! Cheers are a song to their ears. **4**

Stop and Think

4 Why do dancers like to hear people cheer?

Dancers like to hear people cheer because _____

_____

_____

185

Plan a Performance

A performance will be a real treat for all.
First, pick the song. Then, plan taps, leaps
and skips that go with the beat. The beat may
be fast, or it may be slow. You'll just need to
feel that beat. **5**

Stop and Think

5 What are the kids planning? Look at the heading to
find out.

The kids are planning _____

_____

Leap and spin! Tap and skip! Concentrate on the tune, and match the beat. It's hard work, but keep it up! You want your performance to be the best. And when it's over, you will feel relieved! **6**

Stop and Think

6 What are three places where people can keep the beat?

People can keep the beat _____

_____

At last! Moms and dads are in their seats.
You leap! You skip! You tap and spin!
The people shout! They cheer! They
stomp their feet! Now they see how you can
keep that beat! **7**

Stop and Think

7 How do you know the people like the
performance?

I know they like the performance because _____
_____

© Harcourt

Think Critically

1. What does the author want you to learn from this selection? AUTHOR'S PURPOSE

The author wants me to learn _____

_____

_____

2. What will make a good performance? CAUSE AND EFFECT

A performance will be good if _____

_____

_____

3. What are three reasons that people keep the beat? Copy the chart, and fill it in. MAIN IDEA AND DETAILS

```
            ┌──────────────────────────────────────┐
            │  Reasons That People Keep the Beat    │
            └──────────────────────────────────────┘
              /                │                  \
   ┌──────────────┐   ┌──────────────┐   ┌──────────────┐
   │              │   │              │   │              │
   └──────────────┘   └──────────────┘   └──────────────┘
```

committee

crop

earn

experiments

provide

supplies

Vocabulary

Build Robust Vocabulary

Read the selection and think about the meanings of the words in dark type.

John Muir liked to be outside. He wanted to **earn** a living as a farmer. He got **supplies** like rakes and hoes. Then he planted each **crop.** He planted fruit trees and grape vines. John did **experiments** to make his fruit taste different. He always used the land with respect.

John wanted to make a park to protect some land. The park would **provide** us with a spot that we all could use. A **committee** met and talked with John about his plans for a park.

Write the Vocabulary Word that completes each sentence. The first one has been done for you.

1. John got _____ **supplies** _____ to help him farm the land.

2. John had to _____ a living, so he became a farmer.

3. One _____ he planted was fruit trees.

4. In his _____ , John made the fruit taste different.

5. A _____ met with John to talk.

6. A park can _____ us with a spot that we all can use.

His Land Is Our Land

by Chase Parr

illustrated by Alexander Farquharson

When John Muir was small, his family had a farm. Farm work was hard. He found this work suited him because he liked to be outside. He could hear birds sing and watch the animals around him. He could rest beside the calm water of a lake. John liked to do these things in his extra time. **1**

Stop and Think

1 What do you learn from the title of this story?

From the title, I learn that _____

_____

_____

When John was bigger, he left home. He found work to do. He could earn cash to take care of his bills. He made a home for himself.

Then John got hurt at his job. He could not see for a while. He had to rest for a long time and get better. When he could see again, John made a rule. He would travel and spend all of his time outside. **2**

Stop and Think

2 **What happened after John left home?**

After John left home, he _____

_____

_____

John wanted to see the land, but where would he go? He didn't know. But he made one rule for his trip. He would not stop until he got to the spot that suited him best.

John chose to hike the hills in the East. He got supplies for his trip and left. **3**

© Harcourt

194

After that trip, John wanted to go to other spots. He traveled west into the hills. Here, he found blue lakes and streams with clean water. There were tall trees and many animals. John liked this spot and chose to spend some time there. **4**

Stop and Think

4 **Why do you think the author wrote about John?**

I think the author wrote about John because

_____

_____

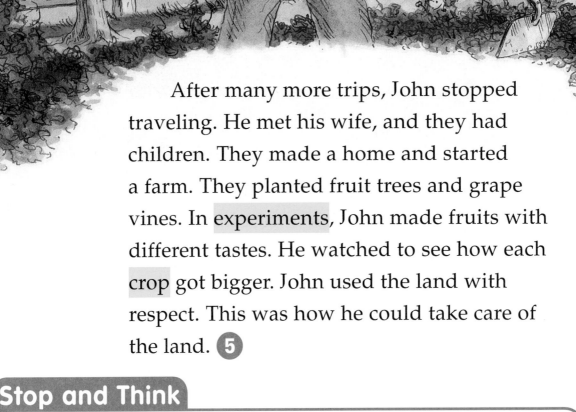

After many more trips, John stopped traveling. He met his wife, and they had children. They made a home and started a farm. They planted fruit trees and grape vines. In experiments, John made fruits with different tastes. He watched to see how each crop got bigger. John used the land with respect. This was how he could take care of the land. **5**

Stop and Think

5 **What did John do after he stopped traveling?**

After he stopped traveling, John _____

_____

_____

Around him, John could see clues that
people were not taking care of the land. John
remembered the land from his travels. He
remembered what the land was like before a
lot of people had arrived. He wanted some
of this land to become a park. A park could
be protected. It would provide us with a spot
that we all could use. The park would have
rules to keep it safe. **6**

Stop and Think

6 Do you think John's plan for the land was wise or
foolish? Explain your answer.

I think his plan for the land was _____

_____

Would anyone agree with John? An important committee met to settle how the land would be used. Would it be used for homes and mines? Would it be made into a park? They agreed with John. The land would be made into a park.

Now we can visit this park. Thanks to John Muir, this land will be safe forever. **7**

Stop and Think

7 What happened because of John's work?

Because of John's work, _____

_____

_____

Think Critically

1. What happens in the story? Copy the chart, and fill it in. **SEQUENCE**

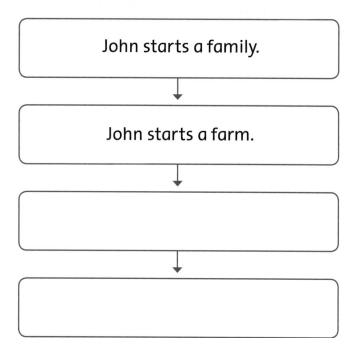

> John starts a family.

> John starts a farm.

2. How would you describe John Muir? **CHARACTER**

John Muir is _____

_____

3. What is the main idea of this story? **MAIN IDEA AND DETAILS**

The main idea of the story is _____

_____

Vocabulary

Build Robust Vocabulary

Write the word that best completes each sentence. The first one has been done for you.

1. In this game, one player gives hints. The rest of the players are all _____**sleuths**_____ .

       sleuths   hosts   statues

2. You can't make a mistake. You must

_____ tell what the

instead   except   accurately

player is acting out.

3. A man asks who will go first. One player

_____ by jumping up.

responds   risks   earns

4. One player is as still as a

_____ .

host   sleuth   statue

5. The _____ keeps the show

       sleuth   host   statue

going. He talks to the players.

6. You _____ missing the fun if

      respond   earn   risk

you do not play!

What Am I?

by Sandra Widener
illustrated by Jan Bryan Hunt

Cast of Characters

Narrator	Player 2
Host	Player 3
Player 1	Audience

Narrator: Let's all clap now!

Host: I'm the host of "What Am I?"

Audience: Let's play!

Host: This is the game. One player pretends to be something. He or she gives hints. You are the sleuths. If you accurately say what that player is, you win. **1**

Stop and Think

1 How many players are in the game?

In this game there are _____

_____

_____

Audience: Okay! Time to play!

Host: Player 1, will you go first?

Narrator: Player 1 responds. She jumps up, bends over, and inches along.

Player 1: I am so slow. What am I?

Player 2: Hmmm. Are you an inchworm?

Audience: Good one! **2**

Stop and Think

2 What is the setting of this play?

The setting of this play is _____

_____

_____

Player 1: No! Here is a hint. I have no tail.

Player 3: No tail?

Audience: No tail!

Player 2: Do you eat hay?

Player 1: I do not. I eat plants in a garden. 3

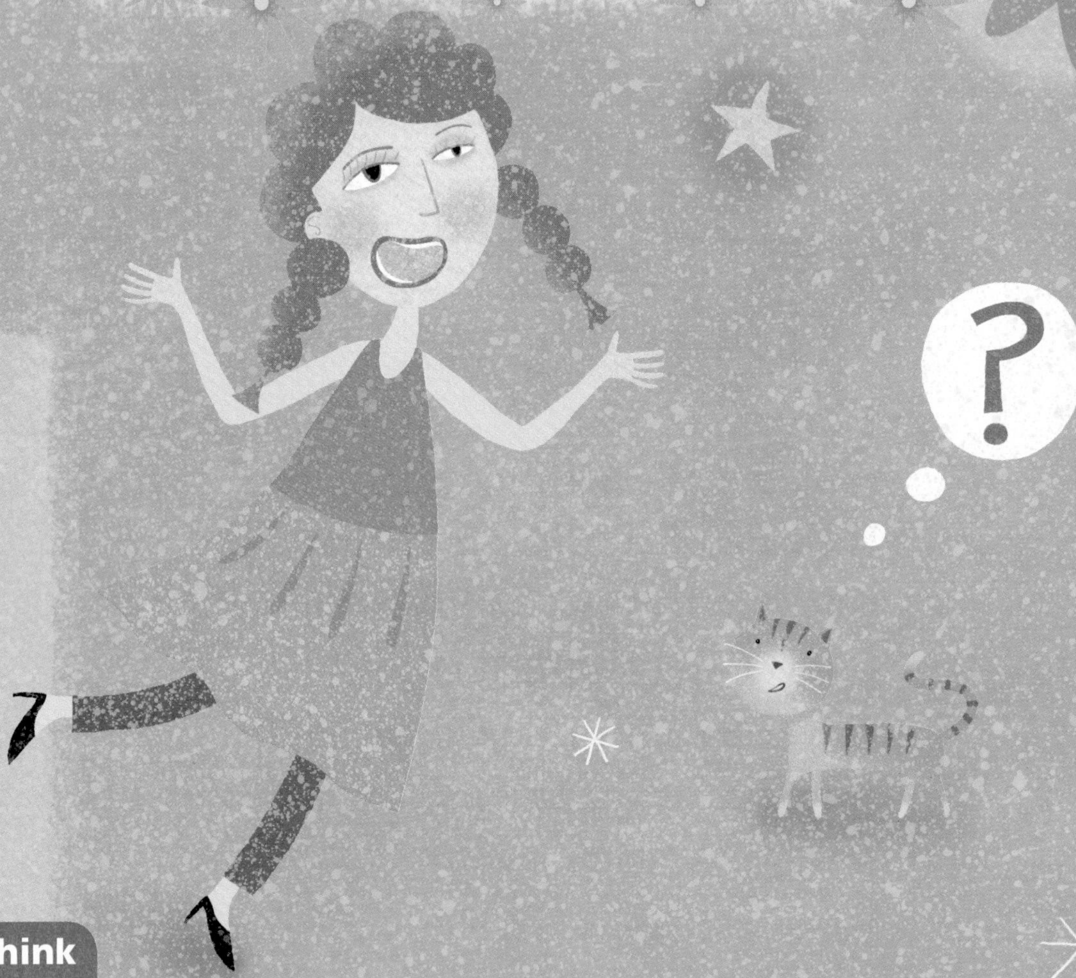

Stop and Think

3 What do you think Player 1 is pretending to be?

I think Player 1 is pretending to be ______________

____

____

Narrator: No tail. Does not eat hay. Eats plants. What could she be?

Player 1: I'll give you two more hints. I'm gray. And I travel on slime!

Audience: Yuck!

Player 2: I think I know!

Host: Yes? What is she, Player 2?

Player 2: Are you a snail?

Player 1: Yes, I am! But it pains me to say that no one likes me. **4**

Stop and Think

4 Why does Player 2 think Player 1 is a snail?

Player 2 thinks Player 1 is a snail because _____

_____

_____

Player 3: Other snails like you a lot!

Narrator: The crowd claps!

Host: Very good! Player 2, you are next.

Narrator: Player 2 runs to the front.

Player 2: You pay to jump on me. You wait for me. You have to watch the time or risk missing me!

Player 3: Are you a plane?

Audience: Good one! **5**

Stop and Think

5 Why does Player 3 think Player 2 is a plane?

Player 3 thinks Player 2 is a plane because _____

_____

_____

Player 2: No, not a plane!

Host: Player 2, give more hints.

Player 2: Sometimes I am as still as a statue. Sometimes I go fast.

Player 1: A dog?

Player 3: You do not pay to jump on a dog!

Player 1: Yes, yes. I forgot.

Player 3: Are you a horse?

Player 2: You do not wait for a horse! **6**

Stop and Think

6 What hints has Player 2 given?

These are the hints Player 2 has given: _____

_____

_____

Player 1: Can we get another hint?

Host: We are out of time! We can't wait much longer! Can anyone help us?

Audience: Player 2 is a train!

Host: Right! Come back and play the game with us next week! **7**

Stop and Think

7 Who figures out Player 2's hints? Underline the words that tell you.

The people who figure out Player 2's hints are

_____

© Harcourt

Think Critically

1. What are the rules for this game? **MAIN IDEA AND DETAILS**

The rules for this game are _____

_____

_____

2. What is the host's job? **CHARACTER**

The host's job is to _____

_____

3. How do you know the author wrote this play to entertain you? **AUTHOR'S PURPOSE**

I know the author wrote this play to entertain

me because _____

_____

bargain

boost

comfortable

delivered

exchanged

spoiled

Vocabulary

Build Robust Vocabulary

Write the Vocabulary Word that completes each sentence. The first one has been done for you.

1. Pam likes to _____**boost**_____ Jo up to swing.

2. Pam's day was _____ when

Jo got sick.

3. Pam wanted to make Jo _____

in her bed.

4. Miss Bolt and Pam _____ hellos.

5. They made a _____ .

Miss Bolt would pay Pam to clean her shop.

6. Emma said stuffed animals would help.

She _____ some to Pam's home.

**Write the Vocabulary Word that best
completes the synonym web.**

7.

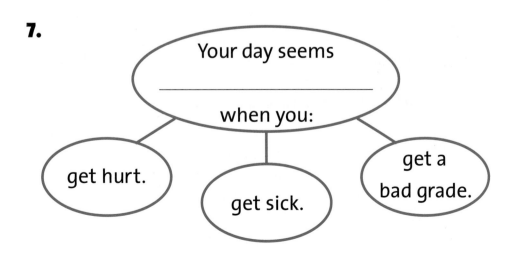

Your day seems
_____
when you:

get hurt.

get sick.

get a
bad grade.

Pam's Big Plan

by Ben Okoji

illustrated by Sarah Dillard

My sister Jo and I are pals. We both like to go outside. We have a big swing that we play on. I boost Jo up onto it, and we sit and tell wild tales. When it's hot, we go to the pond. When it's cold, we don't mind. We still go out. **1**

Stop and Think

1 **What do Jo and Pam like to do?**

Jo and Pam like to _____

_____

_____

One day, Jo felt sick. "I don't want to go out," she told me. I could not make Jo smile. But I could make her comfortable. So I did.

"Mom," I said, "Jo feels bad! What can we do?"

"Jo has a cold," Mom told me. "She'll feel fine in a day or so."

I moped. I missed Jo. Without her, my day was spoiled. **2**

Stop and Think

2 **What problems do Jo and Pam have?**

Jo's problem is _____

Pam's problem is _____

_____

213

I sat. Then I made a plan. I told Mom.
She told me, "That's a fine plan! Let's go
see Miss Bolt. She can help."

So we went to see Miss Bolt. Miss Bolt
and I exchanged hellos. Then I told her my
plan. She and I made a bargain. She let me
clean up the shop while she sold gold rings.
Then she would pay me. **3**

Stop and Think

3 Miss Bolt and Pam make a bargain. Why is this a
bargain?

It is a bargain because _____

_____

Then I went to see Mrs. Davis. She was taking care of her wild roses.

"Hi, Mrs. Davis!" I said.

"How are you, Pam?" Mrs. Davis asked.

"I'm fine," I told her. "But Jo is sick." Then I told Mrs. Davis my plan.

Mrs. Davis said, "I'd like to help." She gave me some roses to take home.

"Thanks!" I said. **4**

Stop and Think

4 **What do you think Pam's plan is?**

I think Pam's plan is to _____

_____

_____

© Harcourt

Next, I went to find Emma. "Jo is sick," I said. I told her my plan.

"I'll help," Emma told me. "These stuffed animals will be good." Then, she delivered them to my home!

"Thanks!" I had one more stop. **5**

Stop and Think

5 **Who is in this story?**

These are the characters in the story: _____

_____

_____

At home, I got my cash. Mom and I went
to the store. Mom helped me find tea and
cold milk. She helped me find the kind of
rolls Jo likes. I got out my cash and gave it to
the clerk. Then we went home. **6**

Stop and Think

6 **What do you think Pam will do with the things
she buys?**

I think Pam will _____

_____

217

I put the roses in a vase. I set out tea, milk, and rolls. I set out the stuffed animals. Then I went to find Jo.

"I have a treat for you!" I said.

"What is it?" she asked. She came out. Then she gasped. "This is so wonderful!" she told me. "You are the best!" We sat and had our tea and rolls. "I feel much better now," Jo said. **7**

Stop and Think

7 What do you think Jo likes best about the party?

I think what Jo likes best is _____

_____

_____

Think Critically

1. How does Jo feel at the end of the story? Why?

CAUSE AND EFFECT

At the end of the story, Jo feels _____

_____

_____

2. Pam is a nice person. How do you know?

CHARACTER

I know she is nice because _____

_____

3. How does the story end? Copy the chart, and fill it in. **PLOT**

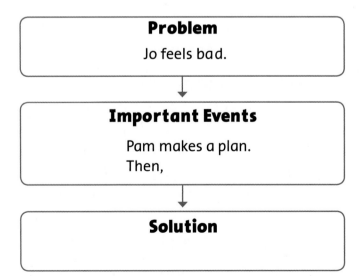

Problem

Jo feels bad.

↓

Important Events

Pam makes a plan.
Then,

↓

Solution

admit

barely

extremely

hilarious

serious

witty

Vocabulary

Build Robust Vocabulary

Read the story and think about the meanings of the words in dark type.

Life on Farmer Sly's farm was just too boring. Farmer Sly had to **admit** that he wanted a little fun. He started to write jokes. "These are **extremely** good!" Farmer Sly said to himself. "These jokes are **hilarious**! They will make my cows laugh."

But the cows did not think Farmer Sly was **witty**. "These are **barely** jokes at all!" the cows said. "We have to stop him! This is **serious**."

Write the Vocabulary Word that completes each sentence. The first one has been done for you.

1. The cows did not think Farmer Sly was

_____**witty**_____ at all.

2. Farmer Sly said his jokes were

_____ good.

3. Farmer Sly said his jokes were so

_____ , they would

make his cows laugh.

4. The cows said Farmer Sly's jokes were

_____ jokes at all.

5. The cows said they must stop Farmer Sly.

They were _____ .

6. Farmer Sly had to _____

that he wanted to have some fun.

FUN FARM

by
Stanley Green

illustrated by Tim Nihoff

Not much went on at Blue Sky Farm.
The sky stayed blue. The grass stayed green.
When a fly buzzed by, that was news.

Farmer Sly felt bored. "I think my life
could be more fun," he told his cows.

"I'll try telling jokes," Farmer Sly said.
But my, those jokes were bad. They made
Farmer Sly's cows cry. **1**

Stop and Think

1 **Why is Farmer Sly bored?**

Farmer Sly is bored because _____

_____

_____

"We can write better jokes than these," the cows said. And they did. But cows are shy. They didn't tell those witty jokes. They tacked them to the posts.

Farmer Sly found the jokes. "These are extremely good!" he said. "They are hilarious! I'll tell them to my friends!"

Farmer Sly's friends liked the jokes, too. **2**

Stop and Think

2 How do you know the author wrote this story to make you laugh?

I know this because _____

_____

One morning, a man called Farmer Sly. He invited Farmer Sly to tell his jokes in a town far away.

"Why not?" said Farmer Sly. He had to admit that he wanted to try.

"My dear cows!" Farmer Sly said. "I am going away. If my jokes are good, I may not be back for a long time." **3**

Stop and Think

3 Why is Farmer Sly going away?

Farmer Sly is going away because _____

_____

_____

When Farmer Sly went onstage, he could not remember the cows' jokes.

"Oh, no!" he said. "All I can think of are my jokes!" So Farmer Sly told his jokes.

"Those are barely jokes at all!" a man said. "Tell us some good jokes."

"No one likes my jokes," Farmer Sly said. "Telling jokes is not for me. I just want to get back to my Blue Sky Farm!" 4

Stop and Think

4 What do you think will happen next?

I think _____

_____

_____

When Farmer Sly got home, he went to see the cows.

"I had my try at telling jokes," he told them. "Too bad they were my jokes and not yours!" Farmer Sly felt sad.

The cows felt sad, too. Blue Sky Farm was now a sad and serious spot. **5**

Stop and Think

5 Who is in this story? Where does the story take place?

The characters are _____

The story takes place at _____

The cows didn't like to see Farmer Sly sad. "We have to make him laugh," one cow said. "But how?"

"I know!" another cow said. "We will write more jokes!"

So they did. Then the cows began to smile. "My, my!" one said. "We write hilarious jokes!" **6**

Stop and Think

6 **Why do the cows feel better now?**

The cows feel better because _____

_____

_____

The cows found Farmer Sly sitting by the pond. They told him their new jokes. Farmer Sly began to laugh. Then he laughed more and clapped his hands.

"My, my! Those are such good jokes!" he said. "Thank you, my dear cows. Those jokes are just what I needed. I give you my word. I will never leave Blue Sky Farm again. And I will never tell my jokes again. Just yours!" **7**

Stop and Think

7 How does Farmer Sly feel at the end of the story?

At the end of the story, _____

_____

_____

Think Critically

1. Why do you think Farmer Sly forgets the cows' jokes at the club? **MAKE INFERENCES**

I think he forgets the jokes because _____

_____

2. How is Farmer Sly different at the end of the story? **MAKE COMPARISONS**

At the end, he _____

_____

3. What happens in the story? Copy the chart, and fill it in. **PLOT**

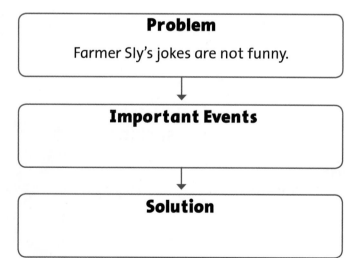

Problem
Farmer Sly's jokes are not funny.

↓

Important Events

↓

Solution

© Harcourt

attack

carefully

crowd

disappear

pattern

sealed

Vocabulary

Build Robust Vocabulary

Write the Vocabulary Word that completes each sentence. The first one has been done for you.

1. Lots of ants _____**crowd**_____ into their small nest.

2. The queen ant is _____ inside the nest. She does not come out.

3. This ant is _____ sucking sap from a plant.

4. The leaves have a _____ of lines. The sap is inside the lines.

© Harcourt

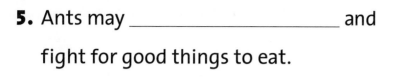

5. Ants may _____ and

fight for good things to eat.

6. Then the ants _____

back into their nest.

**Write the answers to these questions.
Use complete sentences.**

7. Where do ants crowd?

_____

_____

8. What do ants do when they attack?

_____

_____

9. What kind of pattern do leaves have?

_____

_____

Ants

by Stanley Green

 Look at the ants! They are all over. Ants might be red, brown, or black. There are more than nine thousand kinds of ants. They feel right at home in almost any spot.

Ants crowd into their nest. A nest might be in a hole. In their nest, the ants are out of sight. You might see ants walking around in bright light. They are looking for food. Soon, they disappear back into their nest. **1**

Stop and Think

1 **What do you know about ants so far?**

This is what I know about ants so far: _____

_____

_____

Some ants like to march. They march in a long line. They walk right over anything in their path. If it's good to eat, they attack and fight it. Then they march on until they find something else to eat. **2**

Stop and Think

2 How do you know that the author wrote this selection to give you facts?

I know this because _____

_____

© Harcourt

trunk

pincers

end

An ant has three parts. On the first part are two pincers. An ant picks up food with them and digs with them. The mouth is near these.

The trunk is the second part. There are three legs on each side. Some ants have wings. The wings have a pattern of lines.

What is the biggest part of an ant? The biggest part is right at the end. This part might have a stinger. **3**

Stop and Think

3 Look at the diagram. Where are the wings?

The wings are _____

_____

_____

© Harcourt

Ants eat many kinds of food. Some ants eat parts of plants. Other ants carefully suck sap from plants. And some ants eat the eggs of other bugs. At night, most ants are sleeping in their nests. **4**

Stop and Think

4 **What are three things ants will eat?**

Three things ants will eat are _____

_____

_____

Good
spot for
a nest!

An ant's life starts with a queen. The queen finds a good spot for a nest. She digs the nest deep in the ground. The nest is safe and out of sight.

The queen is sealed inside her nest. Her job is to lay eggs. **5**

Stop and Think

5 What do you think you will learn about next?

I think I will learn _____

_____

_____

Most of the eggs hatch into worker ants. Worker ants watch over new eggs. They take care of the queen night and day. They might live for ten weeks. The queen keeps laying eggs. She might live for twenty years.

Sometimes, a new queen is born. The new queen and many males will fly away. The new queen looks for the right spot to make her nest. **6**

Stop and Think

6 **What do worker ants do?**

Worker ants _____

_____

_____

 The old queen stays right in the old nest. Worker ants stay there with her. Life stays the same for them. In the dark, out of sight, the ants go on with their lives. **7**

Stop and Think

7 What happens in a queen's life?

In a queen's life, she _____

_____

_____

Think Critically

1. Why does a queen ant never leave her nest?
CAUSE AND EFFECT

A queen ant never leaves her nest because

_____

_____

2. How is a queen ant different from a worker
ant? **MAKE COMPARISONS**

A queen ant _____

_____

_____

3. What have you learned about ants? Copy the
chart, and fill it in. **MAIN IDEA AND DETAILS**

K	W	L
What I Know	**What I Want to Know**	**What I Learned**

blended

cradled

crumpled

distance

personalities

raggedy

Vocabulary

Build Robust Vocabulary

Read the selection and think about the meanings of the words in dark type.

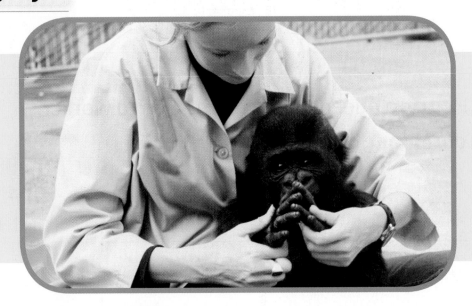

At a far **distance,** all apes might look alike. But they are not the same. Different apes have different **personalities.**

Penny wanted to teach a baby ape named Koko. You might think a baby gorilla would be **raggedy,** but Koko was cute. Koko **blended** in easily with new surroundings. She was very easy to teach.

One day, Penny gave Koko a kitten. Koko **cradled** her new pal like a baby. Koko **crumpled** paper and watched the kitten play with it.

© Harcourt

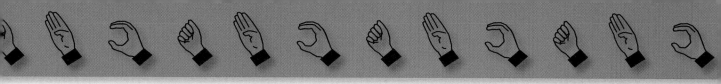

Write the Vocabulary Word that completes each sentence. The first one has been done for you.

1. Apes might look alike from a far
_____**distance**_____ .

2. Koko was cute, not _____ .

3. Koko _____ paper so the
kitten could play with it.

4. Koko _____ the kitten
in her arms.

5. All apes do not act the same. They have
different _____ .

6. Koko fit in well. She _____ in
easily with her new surroundings.

Tell Me

by Sandra Widener

Penny watched the baby ape named Koko. You might think a baby gorilla would be raggedy, but Koko was cute and tiny. She was exactly what Penny had hoped to find.

Different animals have different personalities. Some animals blend in easily with new surroundings. Penny felt that an animal like this would be easy to teach. Koko might be one of them. **1**

Stop and Think

1 Who is Penny?

Penny is _____

_____

_____

Penny got to work. First, she gave Koko a drink. Then, Penny used her hand to say *drink*. She gave the baby ape something to eat. Then she used her hand to say *food*. She did this again and again.

Within two weeks, Koko started to copy Penny. She used her hand to say *drink*. Penny was right. Teaching Koko was easy. **2**

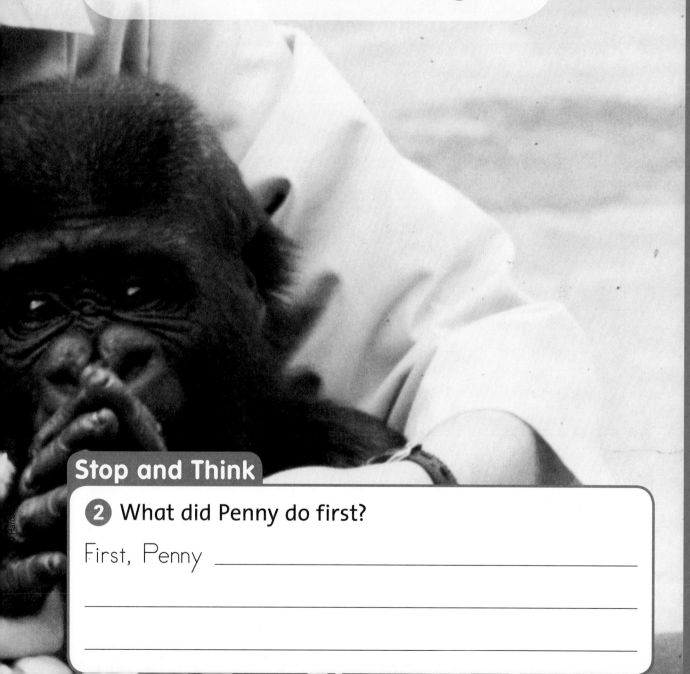

Stop and Think

2 **What did Penny do first?**

First, Penny _____

_____

_____

k

o

k

o

Before long, Koko could use many words. Then Koko put words together. She put together *pour that drink hurry hurry*. Koko was almost chatty!

Penny was happy. She felt lucky. Koko was smart! Penny began to teach Koko more and more words. **3**

Koko signs the word *listen*.

Stop and Think

3 Why is Penny happy?

Penny is happy because _____

_____

_____

One day, Koko said something new with her hand. She said the same thing over and over. Penny watched closely. What did Koko want? Koko wanted a kitten.

So Penny got Koko a fluffy baby kitten. Koko was really happy! She named her kitten All Ball. She cradled him like a baby. **4**

k
i
t
t
y

Stop and Think

4 Why does Penny get Koko a kitten?

Penny gets Koko a kitten because_____

_____

_____

Koko signs the word *sad*.

 f
 r
 o
 w
 n

Koko spent lots of time with her kitty. Koko crumpled paper and tossed it some distance. She would watch All Ball play with it for a long time.

But then something sad happened. All Ball died. Koko was filled with grief. Penny was sad, too. How could she help Koko? **5**

Stop and Think

5 **What do you think will happen next?**

Next, _____

_____

_____

Koko signs the word *Smoky*.

Koko signs the word *love*.

Finally, Penny got Koko two new fluffy kittens. Koko still missed her buddy All Ball. But the new pets made her happy again. Koko named one kitten Smoky. She named the other one Lipstick. **6**

l

o

v

e

Stop and Think

6 Why is Koko happy now?

Koko is happy now because _____

_____

_____

p
a
l
s

Many years have passed. Koko is no longer a baby ape. She is a big gorilla. But Koko and Penny are still friends. Koko is still chatty. She has plenty to say.

To this day, Penny's work with Koko is studied closely. Koko still has much to tell us about how apes think. **7**

Stop and Think

7 Why do you think people study Koko?

I think people study Koko because _____

_____

_____

Think Critically

1. Think about Koko and her pet kittens. Copy the chart, and fill it in. **SEQUENCE**

```
┌─────────────────────────────────────┐
│  Koko gets her kitten All Ball.      │
└─────────────────────────────────────┘
                  │
                  ▼
┌─────────────────────────────────────┐
│  All Ball dies.                      │
└─────────────────────────────────────┘
                  │
                  ▼
┌─────────────────────────────────────┐
│  Koko is sad.                        │
└─────────────────────────────────────┘
                  │
                  ▼
┌─────────────────────────────────────┐
│                                      │
└─────────────────────────────────────┘
```

2. How does Penny teach Koko to talk? **MAIN IDEA AND DETAILS**

Penny teaches Koko to talk by _____

_____

_____

3. What does the author want you to learn from this selection? **AUTHOR'S PURPOSE**

The author wants me to learn _____

_____

_____

Vocabulary

Build Robust Vocabulary

Write the word that best completes each sentence. The first one has been done for you.

1. It's not _____**feasible**_____ to show all

serious   feasible   comfortable

that farmers do. There is so little time!

2. Farmers have a big job. They have a lot to

_____ .

attend   accomplish   report

3. A man and woman are here to

_____ on the farm.

accomplish   report   attend

They will tell what a farm is like.

4. They talk to farmers from our

_____ .

bargain   area   distance

© Harcourt

5. The farmers _____

          serve   accomplish   attend

meetings with other farmers. They talk

about what works best.

6. Farmers _____ us by

          serve   accomplish   attend

growing things we can eat.

Write the answers to these questions.
Use complete sentences.

7. What do the reporters want to accomplish?

_____

_____

8. How do farmers serve us?

_____

_____

Way to Grow!

by Sandra Widener

illustrated by Diane Greenseid

Cast of Characters

Narrator	Farmer Gates
Farmer Coats	Reporter 1
Farmer Snow	Reporter 2

Reporter 1: We are here to report on farms.

Reporter 2: Meet three farmers from our area.

Reporter 1: They will show us what they grow. **1**

Stop and Think

1 What will you find under the heading "Cast of Characters"?

Under "Cast of Characters," I will find _____

_____

Farmer Coats: How are you? I am fine. I can't wait! Let me show you what I grow.

Narrator: Farmer Snow gives Farmer Coats a look. His look says, "Slow down!"

Farmer Snow: We are glad to be here. We want to show you our farms. Then you can tell others about the work we do.

Farmer Gates: You can tell them that this is where their food comes from. **2**

Stop and Think

2 Why does Farmer Snow want to show the reporters the farms?

He wants to show them because _____

_____

Reporter 1: So what do you do?

Farmer Coats: We grow lots of things you eat. If you serve it, we may just grow it!

Reporter 1: But growing takes a long time.

Reporter 2: Don't you hate to wait when things are slow?

Farmer Snow: No. Plants grow slowly. But farmers have to work quickly. **3**

Stop and Think

3 What has happened so far in the play?

So far in the play, _____

_____

_____

Narrator: The farmers stop and think. What is feasible to show the reporters? They do not have much time.

Farmer Gates: What can we show you?

Farmer Coats: We had better get started!

Narrator: They walk down the road.

Farmer Snow: Do you see these cows?

Farmer Coats: These cows give milk.

Farmer Snow: We make it into cheese. **4**

Stop and Think

4 What do you think will happen next?

Next, I think _____

_____

_____

Farmer Coats: Come down this road.

Farmer Gates: See the rows of plants? They will grow into hay, beans, and oats.

Farmer Coats: We plant beets, potatoes, and corn.

Farmer Snow: We weed the rows.

Farmer Coats: Then when the plants are grown, we pick them. We load them onto trucks and send them to markets. **5**

Stop and Think

5 What have the farmers shared about the farms?

The farmers have told us that _____

_____

_____

Farmer Gates: Fruit grows on our trees.

Farmer Coats: And we pick it, too.

Reporter 1: My! You have a lot to do.

Farmer Snow: But that's not all. We raise goats and show them at fairs.

Farmer Gates: We attend meetings with other farmers. We talk about what works best on our farms. We . . .

Reporter 2: Wait! Stop! **6**

Stop and Think

6 Why does Reporter 2 ask the farmers to stop?

Reporter 2 asks them to stop because _____

_____

_____

All three farmers: Stop? But we haven't finished. There is a lot more we accomplish!

Reporter 1: I know, I know. But just hearing about all you do makes us tired.

Farmer Snow: Okay. You stay here and rest.

Farmer Gates: But we have to go.

Narrator: And so, the reporters end their story. But the farmers are off. They have loads of work to do. **7**

Stop and Think

7 What have you learned about the farmers?

I have learned that the farmers _____

_____

_____

Think Critically

1. How is the job of a reporter different from the job of a farmer? **MAKE COMPARISONS**

A reporter _____

_____

_____

2. What happens at the end of this play? **PLOT**

At the end of the play, _____

_____

_____

3. How do you think the author feels about farmers? **AUTHOR'S PERSPECTIVE**

I think the author _____

_____

_____

fragrant

gently

grunted

pleaded

replied

smothered

Vocabulary

Build Robust Vocabulary

Read the story and think about the meanings of the words in dark type.

"Can we eat?" Bobby **pleaded.**

"Not yet," his dad **replied.**

Bobby's dad **gently** stirred the food with a spoon. Bobby sniffed and **grunted.** He didn't think it would be good.

The food smelled **fragrant.** Mom put in garlic. She **smothered** it with the rest of the food.

Write the Vocabulary Word that completes each sentence. The first one has been done for you.

1. "Can we eat?" Bobby _____ **pleaded** _____
to his dad.

2. The food smelled _____ .

3. Bobby _____ when he
sniffed the food.

4. Dad _____ stirred the food
with care.

5. Bobby's mom _____ the
garlic with more food.

6. Bobby asked if they could eat. His dad
_____ , "Not yet."

Good Cooking

by Chase Parr

illustrated by Johanna van der Sterre

One day at noon, Bobby walked into the kitchen. He was in the mood for food. He stood on a step stool and looked on a shelf.

"There's not much to eat, Mom," he said.

"Don't look now," said Mom, "but here's Dad with bags of food!" **1**

Stop and Think

1 How is Bobby feeling?

Bobby is feeling _____

_____

_____

Mom filled a pot with water and put it on the stove. Bobby stood close by and watched.

Dad held out a box of beans and shook it.

"How about these?" he said. "They'll taste good when they're cooked."

Bobby grunted. He didn't think so.

"You'll see," said Mom. **2**

Stop and Think

2 What do you think they are going to make?

I think they are going to make _____

_____

_____

© Harcourt

Soon, Bobby's friend Ray showed up.
"We're cooking lunch," Bobby said.
"Cool," Ray replied. "I like lunch."
Dad took out a cookbook and looked
at it. Then, plop! He added some carrots to
the beans. He gently stirred the mix with a
wooden spoon. **3**

Stop and Think

3 How are Ray's feelings about lunch different from
Bobby's?

Ray _____

Bobby _____

"Did you know that carrots are roots?" Dad asked.

"I did," said Bobby. "That doesn't make them good."

Bobby and Ray stood and stared at the pot.

"Food doesn't cook any faster if you keep looking at it," Mom said. **4**

4 **What does Bobby think about the carrots?**

Bobby thinks that the carrots _____

_____

_____

Dad took another look at the cookbook.

"Would you like to help cook?" he asked. He gave Bobby a scoop.

"Stand on the step stool," he said. "Add three big scoops of cornmeal."

"Will that make it good?" asked Ray.

"It will," said Mom. "So will these bits of meat." Ray added them as Dad stirred the pot with the wooden spoon. **5**

Stop and Think

5 What does Ray add to the pot? Underline the words that tell you.

Ray adds _____

_____

Bobby's dog Moose came into the room.

"He smells something good," Dad said.

"I don't think so," said Bobby.

"You can't fool a dog," Mom said. "A dog has a good nose."

Moose began to drool. **6**

Stop and Think

6 **Why does Moose drool?**

Moose drools because _____

_____

_____

Soon, they could all smell the fragrant food.

"Can we eat soon?" Bobby pleaded.

"One thing is missing," Mom said. Mom stirred garlic into the pot. She smothered it with the rest of the food.

"Yum!" Bobby said. "This is good!"

"What a surprise!" Mom said. **7**

Stop and Think

7 How do you know the author wrote this story to entertain you?

I know this because _____

_____

© Harcourt

Think Critically

1. Bobby is hungry at first. How is this problem solved? **PLOT**

The problem is solved when _____

_____

_____

2. Why is the food so good? Copy the chart, and fill it in. **CAUSE AND EFFECT**

Cause		Effect
	→	The food is very good.

3. What does Bobby think about the lunch at first? How does this change? **MAKE COMPARISONS**

At first, Bobby thinks _____

_____

Later, Bobby _____

_____

© Harcourt

award
beyond
create
grand
literature
noticed

Vocabulary

Build Robust Vocabulary

Write the Vocabulary Word that completes each sentence. The first one has been done for you.

1. When he was little, Lewis Carroll lived in a big house. It was _____ **grand** _____ .

2. Lewis liked to make up stories. He liked to _____ tales for children.

3. In one story, a girl falls down a rabbit hole. Then she finds a strange world _____ the rabbit hole.

© Harcourt

4. Another writer _____

the story at a friend's home.

5. He knew it was a good story.

He knew it was a work of fine

_____ .

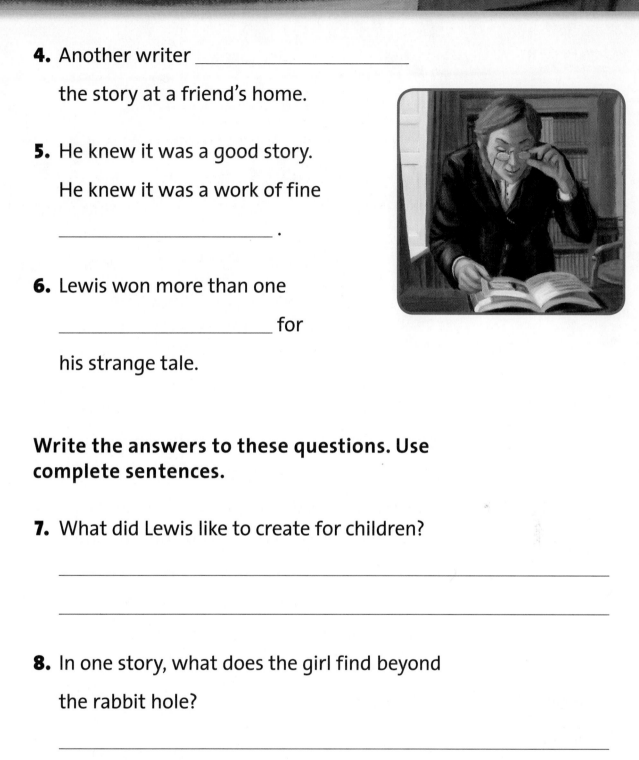

6. Lewis won more than one

_____ for

his strange tale.

Write the answers to these questions. Use complete sentences.

7. What did Lewis like to create for children?

_____

_____

8. In one story, what does the girl find beyond

the rabbit hole?

_____

_____

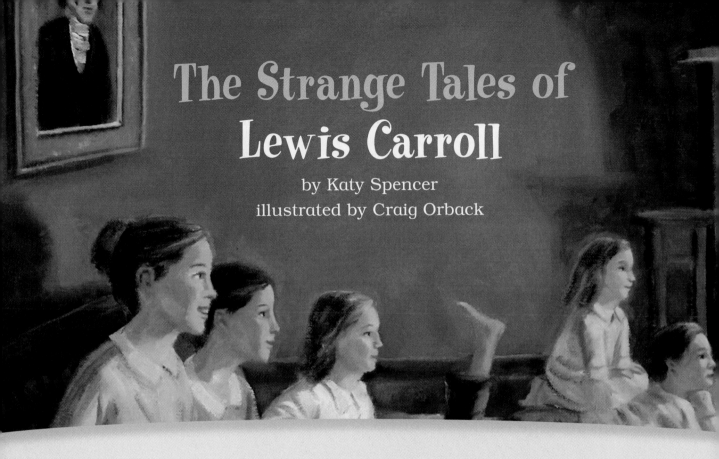

The Strange Tales of Lewis Carroll

by Katy Spencer

illustrated by Craig Orback

Lewis Carroll was born in England in the 1800s. He was part of a large family. They lived in a grand house in a small village.

In those days, there was no TV. Children made up other things to do. From the time he was little, Lewis took charge of making daily life interesting. He liked to create tales of make-believe things. He made up new games for everyone to play. **1**

Stop and Think

1 Why did children have to make up things to do at this time?

Children had to make up things to do because

_____

Lewis also liked to read. He was good at math and knew a lot about numbers. He was very smart.

His parents sent Lewis away to study. When Lewis left home, he worked hard. But he missed his large family. Once again, Lewis took charge. In his extra time, he made up stories and told them to his friends. **2**

Stop and Think

2 **What has happened so far?**

So far, Lewis Carroll _____

_____

_____

In time, Lewis became a teacher. Lewis liked children, but he never had any of his own. So the children of his friends were very important to this gentle man. He would tell them stories. While he was telling his stories, the children would not budge. They didn't want to miss a word. **3**

Stop and Think

3 Why were his friends' children important to Lewis?

His friends' children were important to him because ___

___

___

One day, Lewis took a friend and his
three children on a boating trip. One child
was named Alice. As they went down the
river, Lewis made up a story. In the story, a
girl named Alice fell down a rabbit hole. She
found strange and wonderful things beyond
the rabbit hole. She discovered that she could
change her size. She became as small as a fly
and as big as a giant. **4**

Stop and Think

4 **Why is the girl in Lewis's story called Alice?**

She is called Alice because _____

_____

_____

Alice liked the story. She liked it so much that she asked Lewis to put it on paper. Lewis did, and he made pictures for it, too.

Then another writer noticed the story at Alice's home. He knew the story was good. He knew it was a work of fine literature. He wanted to turn the story into a book that many children would read. **5**

Stop and Think

5 What do you think will happen to Lewis's story?

I think _____

_____

_____

The story Alice liked so much became the book *Alice's Adventures in Wonderland.* It was a big hit.

Lewis's next book was a hit, too! In that book, Alice stepped into the other side of a mirror. There, she had more strange adventures. Each book won more than one award. **6**

Stop and Think

6 Why do you think Lewis's books are a big hit?

Lewis's books are a big hit because _____

_____

_____

Many writers have told tales of wonderful things. But they are not always as interesting, or as well-liked, as those imagined by Lewis Carroll. Children and their parents will be reading his books for ages to come. **7**

Stop and Think

7 Why do you think the author chose to write about Lewis Carroll?

I think she wrote about him because _____

_____

Think Critically

1. Why did Lewis Carroll make up stories?
CHARACTERS' MOTIVATIONS

He made up stories because _____

_____

2. What is the main idea of this biography? MAIN
IDEA AND DETAILS

The main idea is _____

_____

3. How did the biography end? Copy the chart,
and fill it in. SEQUENCE

> Lewis Carroll makes up stories.

↓

> Lewis Carroll goes to school and becomes a teacher.

↓

> Lewis Carroll writes a story about Alice.

↓

> [ ]

collections

common

last

rare

separated

settled

Vocabulary

Build Robust Vocabulary

Read the selection and think about the meanings of the words in dark type.

Some men and women study the past. They dig deep in the ground. They want to find things like **rare** old coins and toys. These things were **common** in homes long ago. They tell us that humans **settled** there.

Some of these digs can **last** for years. The things they find may be **separated** by many layers of dirt. These things can end up in **collections.** Then you can see them, too!

© Harcourt

Write the Vocabulary Word that completes each sentence. The first one has been done for you.

1. Workers may find _____**rare**_____ old coins in the dirt.

2. If you want to see old coins, you can look at them in _____ .

3. Long ago, most homes had coins and toys. They were _____ in homes long ago.

4. Some digs take a long time. They may _____ for years.

5. Things in the ground may be _____ by layers of dirt.

6. Coins and toys in the ground tell us that humans _____ there.

Dig for the Old

by Jean Chase
illustrated by Robert McClurkan

Human beings have lived on this planet for a long time. What do you think life was like long ago? What did houses look like? What games did boys and girls play? What did they eat?

There is a way to find out. Look down. Look in the soil under your feet. You may find clues to life in the past. **1**

Stop and Think

1 Why do people like to find old things?

People like to find old things because _____

_____

_____

© Harcourt

282

It's happened before. Boys and girls playing in the soil have found rare old coins. They have found old toys. They have found points from arrows.

These things are clues. They tell us that humans settled there long ago. They tell us to keep digging. Deep in the soil we may find more clues. **2**

Stop and Think

2 What are some clues to the past that you can find in the ground? Underline the words that tell you.

Some clues you can find are _____

_____

Some men and women study the past. It's their job. They dig in soil and sand. Some digs last for years. The diggers find old toys, coins, and pots. These common things tell a story. They tell about the men, women, and children who used them long ago. **3**

Stop and Think

3 How is your family like families from long ago?

My family _____

_____

_____

The diggers make a map of the soil. The map tells them where they found things. They give each thing a number, and they write that number on the map. If they find a toy deep in the soil, the map shows that. If they find a coin close to the top, the map shows that, too. ④

Stop and Think

④ After scientists dig up items and make a map, what do you think they do next?

I think they _____

_____

The diggers study the things they find. With care, they brush the soil away. They compare things. For example, they look at how deep in the soil each toy was found. Suppose one toy was deep in the soil, and the other was not. This tells the diggers that many years separated the boys and girls who played with these two toys. **5**

Stop and Think

5 Why is it important for scientists to know how deep something is buried?

It is important because _____

_____

Diggers are always finding out new things. They may think that a pot was used just to boil water. Then they find a pot just like it. But a coating of oil is inside this pot. The oil tells the digger that there was a different use for the pot. It is a new fact about life long ago. **6**

Stop and Think

6 What is important about the oil in a pot?

The oil in a pot is important because _____

_____

_____

You don't have to join a dig to study old times. You can look at collections of old coins, tools, toys, and other things. They will tell you what boys and girls played with in the past. They will tell you what life was like a long time ago. **7**

Stop and Think

7 How are museums important in the study of life long ago?

Museums are important because _____

_____

Think Critically

1. Why do people's ideas about the past keep changing? CAUSE AND EFFECT

People's ideas about the past keep changing because _____

_____

_____

2. What do you think the author wants you to learn from this article? AUTHOR'S PURPOSE

The author wants me to learn _____

_____

_____

3. What have you learned about digging for old things? Copy the chart, and fill it in. MAIN IDEA AND DETAILS

K	W	L
What I Know	What I Want to Know	What I Learned

budge

discovery

entire

majestic

peered

scampering

Vocabulary

Build Robust Vocabulary

Write the Vocabulary Word that completes each sentence. The first one has been done for you.

1. Dog did not want to get up. He did not want to ___**budge**___ .

2. Sun _____ down at Dog and made him hot.

3. Then Dog went _____ to Creek as fast as his paws could take him.

290

© Harcourt

4. Dog saw that Creek was cool. He had made

a good _____ .

5. Soon Dog's _____ body

was covered with water.

6. Dog found out that Creek had

_____ powers.

**Write the Vocabulary Word that best
completes the synonym web.**

7.

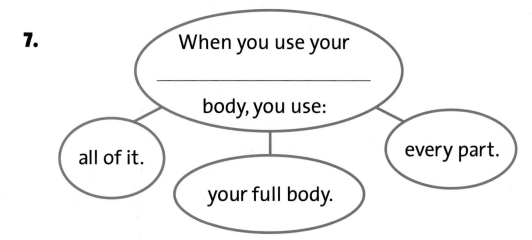

When you use your

_____

body, you use:

all of it.

your full body.

every part.

Dog Asks the Sun

by Sandra Widener

illustrated by Mark Schroder

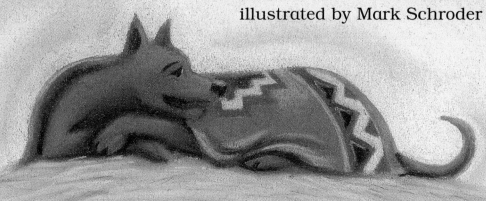

At dawn, Dog woke up and yawned. The air this morning was cold. Dog pulled up a shawl, curled up on his paws, and went back to sleep.

Sun rose up into the sky. Soon, it was almost noon. Still, Dog slept. Dog felt cold on his straw bed. But he did not want to budge. **1**

Stop and Think

1 Where does the story take place?

The story takes place _____

_____

_____

"Sun," Dog called, yawning again.

"Yes?" asked Sun. He peered down and caught sight of Dog. He saw Dog curled up on the straw.

"Sun, I'm cold. Make me warm."

This caught Sun by surprise. Who was this scrawny dog to tell him what to do?

"And warm me as quickly as you can. If you don't mind, that is," Dog added. **2**

Stop and Think

2 **What has happened so far?**

So far, _____

_____

_____

Sun *did* mind. He saw that Dog needed to be taught better manners.

"Yes," Sun said. "I will make you warm." Sun made Dog's straw bed so hot that it almost caught fire.

Dog yelped and jumped out of his straw bed. He went scampering to Creek as fast as his paws would take him. **3**

Stop and Think

3 What does Sun do to teach Dog better manners?

To teach Dog better manners, Sun _____

_____

_____

Dog put his hot paws in Creek's cool water. He had never felt anything so soothing. He was pleased with this discovery.

Creek chuckled at Dog's antics.

Dog lay down in the sand beside Creek. Soon, he was feeling lazy again.

"This is perfect. But I'm awfully thirsty," he said. "Rise up a little. I'd like a drink, but I don't want to budge." **4**

Stop and Think

4 **Why might it be a bad idea for Dog to tell Creek what to do?**

It might be a bad idea because _____

_____

Creek did not chuckle anymore. Now, she frowned. Like Sun, she saw that this lazy dog needed to be taught better manners. So Creek rose, and soon she reached Dog's paws.

"Rise a little more," said Dog.

Soon, Creek reached Dog's jaws.

"Perfect!" said Dog. "You can stop now." **5**

Stop and Think

5 What do you think will happen next?

I think that _____

_____

_____

But Creek didn't stop. She kept rising. Soon, Dog's entire body was covered.

Dog jumped up to run away. But Creek rose faster than Dog's paws could run. Finally, Dog crawled up a tree.

"Oh, this is awful!" Dog cried. "And it's all my fault!" **6**

Stop and Think

6 Why does Creek rise up so high?

Creek rises up so high because _____

_____

_____

He begged Sun and Creek for their help.

"I'm sorry that I tried to tell you what to do," he said. "Please stop the water. Please don't make it so hot. Never again will I forget your majestic powers."

Creek and Sun smiled. They saw that Dog had been taught a lesson. So Creek lowered the water. And Sun dried Dog's fur. **7**

Stop and Think

7 What lesson do you think the author wants you to learn from this story?

I think she wants me to learn _____

_____

Think Critically

1. What does Dog do that makes Sun and Creek angry? **CAUSE AND EFFECT**

Dog _____

_____

2. What is Dog like at the beginning? What is he like at the end? **MAKE COMPARISONS**

At the beginning, Dog is _____

_____

At the end, Dog is _____

_____

3. What happens in the story? Copy the chart, and fill it in. **PLOT**

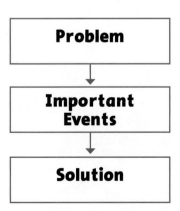

Problem
↓
Important Events
↓
Solution

Vocabulary

Build Robust Vocabulary

Write the word that best completes each sentence. The first one has been done for you.

1. San Francisco is a _____**fantastic**_____ place!

   fragrant   fantastic   common

2. The city's old homes make it a

   _____ place to visit.

   upbeat   spare   historical

3. Coit Tower is an _____ sight.

   smothered   impressive   upbeat

   It sits on top of a hill.

4. On some streets, there is little room to

_____ for cars.

spare   scamper   peer

5. There is a long _____ to get

collection   delay   discovery

on the cable car. But we can wait!

6. Everyone we meet is so

_____ . They make

historical   upbeat   impressive

San Francisco a fun place to be.

**Write the answers to these questions. Use
complete sentences.**

7. What is one impressive sight in San Francisco?

_____

_____

8. Why is there little room to spare on some streets?

_____

_____

The San Francisco File

by Sandra Widener
illustrated by Marilyn Janovitz

Cast of Characters

Lucy	Grace	Percy	Dad	Mom

Grace: Here we are in San Francisco! Since this place was my choice for our trip, I get to record it.

Dad: San Francisco is a fantastic place!

Grace: Mom and Dad are here with me. So is my brother, Percy, and my friend Lucy. Say hello, everyone!

Mom, Dad, Percy, and Lucy: Hello! ①

Stop and Think

① Why does Grace get to record the trip?

Grace gets to record the trip because _____

_____

_____

302

Grace: I'll name things about San Francisco. You tell what you think of them. Percy, how do you like the food?

Percy: I was afraid the food would be too fancy. But it's not. It's very tasty!

Lucy: I liked it, too!

Mom: Last night, the rice had a trace of something spicy. It was so good! ❷

Stop and Think

❷ What do you think the characters will talk about next?

I think the characters will talk about _____

_____

Grace: What about the historical places?

Mom: We visited Coit Tower yesterday.

Dad: That was an impressive sight!

Mom: We could see the whole city.

Percy: And what about Lombard Street! It has so many turns.

Mom: It was so narrow. There was little room to spare as we made each turn. **3**

02:05

02:25

Stop and Think

3 What has happened in the play so far?

So far in this play, _____

_____

_____

Grace: Okay, Lucy. Now is your chance. What do you think of the city?

Lucy: I like the cable cars. There was a long delay to get a ride, and we had to wait. But it was worth it.

Grace: What about shopping?

Lucy: The shopping is wonderful. And everyone we meet is so upbeat. It makes this city a fun place to be! **4**

03:25

03:45

Stop and Think

4 What does Lucy like to do?

Lucy likes to _____

_____

_____

Grace: Dad, your turn. You like art. What kind of art have we seen?

Dad: Yesterday, we went to two museums! Both had beautiful paintings. There was so much to see.

Percy: The museums *were* fun. And lunch at the Pizza Palace was fantastic!

Dad: Percy, you ate four slices! **5**

09:05

01:55

Stop and Think

5 What does the group think of the trip?

The group thinks that _____

_____

_____

Mom: I'd like to get something to remind me of San Francisco.

Dad: Get a nice dress!

Mom: You'd better think twice about that. Remember those high prices? **6**

12:05

05:21

Stop and Think

6 Where does this play take place?

This play takes place _____

_____

_____

Dad: Grace, San Francisco was a good choice. It's been a lot of fun.

Mom: I like San Francisco, too. But it'll be nice to get back home to my own space.

Lucy, Grace, and Percy: There is no place like home!

Stop and Think

7 Why is San Francisco a good place to visit?

San Francisco is a good place to visit because

_____

_____

Think Critically

1. What are some of the things the group does on their trip? **PLOT**

On their trip, the group _____

_____

_____

2. How are the characters in this play alike?

MAKE COMPARISONS

All of the characters _____

_____

_____

3. What do you learn from this play? **AUTHOR'S PURPOSE**

I learn _____

_____

_____